DAY SKIPPER
EXERCISES

QUESTIONS AND ANSWERS

Second edition

PAT LANGLEY-PRICE & PHILIP OUVRY

ADLARD COLES NAUTICAL
London

Acknowledgements

The authors wish to thank Helen Deaves of Stanfords Charts for her assistance in the preparation of the practice chart.

Published by Adlard Coles Nautical
an imprint of A & C Black
Publishers Ltd,
38 Soho Square, London W1D 3HB
www.adlardcoles.com

Copyright © Pat Langley-Price and
Philip Ouvry 1998, 2003

First edition 1998
Reprinted 2001
Second edition 2003
Reprinted 2005

Pat Langley-Price and Philip Ouvry
have asserted their rights under the
Copyright, Designs and Patents Act
1988, to be identified as the authors of
this work.

ISBN–10: 0-7136-6708-7
ISBN–13: 978-0-7136-6708-0

A CIP catalogue record for this book is
available from the British Library.

Typeset in 10.5pt on 12pt Palatino by
Falcon Oast Graphic Art Ltd.

Printed and bound in Great Britain by
The Cromwell Press, Trowbridge,
Wiltshire

Contents

Introduction

Navigation students frequently find difficulty with tidal problems and chartwork. This book of exercises has been prepared as a supplement to the textbook *Day Skipper*. We have assumed that the reader is seeking to extend his knowledge with additional exercises and already has textbooks on small boat navigation. Thus no theoretical explanations are included, though some answers are expanded, where necessary, to give further clarification. To enable the exercises to be completed, all relevant extracts from hydrographic and nautical publications have been included together with the practice chart based on Stanfords Chart 15 with a portion from Stanfords Chart 24. The answers given are set out as model answers, and are complete.

The extracts of pilotage information are principally from the *Macmillan Reeds Nautical Almanac*. The editor of the almanac recommended the use of up-to-date pilotage information which means that there are instances where the data in the extracts may differ from that on the practice chart. These extracts are intended to be examples of the hydrographic information needed by small craft sailors, but it is emphasised that, in practice, an adequate range of publications and charts is required.

Accuracy achieved in theory is often difficult to achieve in real life situations. When doing any navigational exercises, readers should try to make their chartwork as accurate and tidy as possible. However, you will find that much navigational information is inexact, for example: leeway, tidal heights offshore, tidal streams in positions between tidal diamonds. So accurate navigation requires the continued application of the best information available. Most experienced navigators know how much to leave out, but the learner should seek information from as many sources as possible.

Remember that there is no substitute for practical experience. One week spent navigating a boat on a coastal passage is more valuable than a whole winter spent at shorebased theory classes. Having said that, however, we have set out these exercises to enable you to practise your chartwork so that you can navigate with confidence and experience many years of safe sailing.

Pat Langley-Price and Philip Ouvry

Definitions

Chart Datum The reference level on charts. Soundings are given below chart datum. Heights of tide are heights above chart datum.

Course The direction in which the boat is heading. True (T), magnetic (M), and compass (C) courses are the angles between the boat's fore and aft line and the direction of true, magnetic and compass north respectively (measured clockwise from north).

Course To Steer The compass course to be steered by the helmsman. It is found by calculation or by plotting a vector diagram allowing for tidal stream, leeway, variation and deviation.

Depth The vertical distance between sea level and the seabed.

Distance Made Good The distance travelled over the ground taking into account the boat's course and speed, tidal stream and leeway.

Drying Height The height above chart datum of any feature which is covered and uncovered by the tide. Drying heights are underlined on the chart.

Duration Of Tide The period of time between high water and low water for a falling tide, and low water and high water for a rising tide.

Ground Track The track made good over the ground allowing for the boat's course and speed, tidal stream and leeway.

Heading The direction of the boat's fore and aft line.

Height The heights of natural features are given in metres above MHWS. In the case of a light the height is between the focal plane of the light and MHWS.

Height Of Tide The vertical distance between sea level and chart datum at any instant.

Interval The period of time between any instant and the preceding or following HW or LW.

Leeway The sideways drift of a boat caused by the wind. Often expressed as the angle between the course and the water track, and most easily measured astern by observing the angle between the fore and aft line (the reciprocal of the boat's heading) and her wake. The leeway angle is normally between 5° and 10° when the boat is close-hauled depending on the underwater profile of the boat. Bilge keeled boats make more leeway than fin keeled boats. Leeway decreases progressively as the boat bears away to a beam reach, becoming nil when she is running. Leeway has to be taken into account when determining a course to steer and when plotting a water track.

Mean High Water Springs (MHWS), Mean Low Water Springs (MLWS), Mean High Water Neaps (MHWN), Mean Low Water Neaps (MLWN) The mean throughout the year of the heights above chart datum of all HW and LW spring and neap tides.

Range The difference in metres between the heights of HW and the preceding or succeeding LW.

Rise Of Tide At any instant the vertical distance of sea level above LW.

Sounding The (charted) depth of the seabed below chart datum.

Speed Made Good The speed made good over the ground taking into account the boat's course and speed, tidal stream and leeway.

Tidal Stream

Set The direction towards which a tidal stream or current flows.

Rate The speed at which a tidal stream runs, given in knots and tenths of a knot.

Drift The distance that a boat is carried by a tidal stream or current in a given time when no other factors are considered.

Track Made Good The mean track actually achieved over the ground by a boat during a given period of time.

Water Track The track travelled through the water allowing for the effect of leeway (but not tidal stream).

Notes on Exercises

1 Deviation taken from the compass deviation table (Fig 4.1) is to the nearest whole degree.
2 Approximations are made to the nearest tenth of a knot, tenth of a metre in height or depth, tenth of a nautical mile and to the nearest minute in time and degree in angle.
3 A practice chart based on Stanfords Charts 15 and 24 is included with the book.
4 Soundings are, by definition, corrected for height of tide.
5 Buoys are not usually visible at distances over one mile and should be used for bearings only if no suitable landmarks are available.
6 In several instances, courses to steer and estimated time of arrival (ETA) are calculated to a harbour breakwater rather than to the centre of the harbour.
7 There are instances where the data shown in the port information is more up-to-date than that shown on the practice chart.
8 The practice chart is printed in single colour so depth contours are not shown. Depth contours need to be estimated from the depths shown on the chart.

Symbols and Abbreviations

$+$ Dead reckoning position (DR). Position derived only from course steered and distance travelled.

△   Estimated position (EP). Position derived from course steered, distance travelled, leeway and tidal stream.

⊙   Fix. Position derived by direct reference to terrestrial landmarks.

→ Water track.

→› Ground track.

→›› Tidal stream.

‹‹ →› Transferred position line.

BST	British Summer Time (Greenwich Mean Time plus one hour)
C	Compass bearing or course
CD	Chart datum
E	East
ETA	Estimated time of arrival
GMT	Greenwich Mean Time or Universal Time
h	Hours
HW	High water
k	Knots
LW	Low water
M	Magnetic bearing or course, or miles
m	Metres or minutes
MHWS	Mean high water springs
N	North
S	South
s	Seconds
T	True bearing or course
TSS	Traffic Separation Scheme
UT	Universal Time (same as GMT)
VHF	Very High Frequency (radiotelephone)
W	West

1 • Chart Familiarisation

Use chart 15

1.1 The title of the chart is Dorset harbours and approaches. What area does it cover?

1.2 Is the scale the same on the chartlets 2 St Alban's Ledge and 1 Weymouth and Portland?

1.3 What type of projection is chart 15? What is it important to remember about this type of projection?

1.4 What are cautions?

1.5 What do the following abbreviations mean: bkSh R Wd; soM fS; G cS P bkSh?

1.6 Identify the symbols in the following positions:

a) 50° 30'.8N 2° 20'.1W
b) 50° 34'.8N 2° 03'.5W
c) 50° 38'.7N 1° 55'.9W

1.7 What does the following symbol mean: ◇?

1.8 Tabulations for tidal diamonds are referred to a HW at a standard port.

a) What is the standard port for St Alban's Head?
b) What is the standard port for Poole Bay?

1.9 What is the significance of the words *foul ground* bordered by pecked lines close inshore in Poole Bay?

1.10 What is the significance of the magenta rectangle around Christchurch Harbour?

2 • Buoys and Lights

Use chart 15

2.1 Describe the buoy in position 50º 42'.9N 1º 44'.6W.

2.2 Is Anvil Point light visible in Swanage Bay?

2.3 In poor visibility a boat observes several buoys but cannot determine their colour. However, their topmarks are visible.

What type of buoy does each topmark represent?

2.4 A boat is on a northerly course. The navigator is expecting to see an East cardinal buoy ahead. A tall pillar shaped buoy is visible but it has lost its topmark. How can the navigator confirm that this is an East cardinal buoy? On which side should the boat pass?

2.5 Describe the light marking the end of 'C' Head on the north side of the North Ship Channel to Portland Inner Harbour.

2.6 a) Describe an isolated danger mark.
b) Is there one in Studland Bay near Poole Harbour entrance?

2.7 What is a sectored light?

2.8 What is the difference between occulting and flashing? What is an isophase light?

2.9 When travelling in the direction of buoyage, upon which side of the boat will a starboard hand mark be? Describe a starboard hand mark. How do you know which is the direction of buoyage?

2.10 Where can you find the description of a particular lighthouse?

EXERCISES

3 • Position and Direction

Use chart 15

3.1 Measure the latitude and longitude of the following:

   a) Fl Y 2s DZ 'A' buoy off St Alban's Ledge.
   b) W Shambles Q(9) 15s buoy southeast of Portland.
   c) The anchorage symbol off Chesil Cove west of Portland.
   d) Fl Y 2s buoy southeast of Weymouth.
   e) Historic Wreck Fl Y 5s northeast of Bar Buoy No 1 marking the beginning of Swash Channel, Poole Harbour entrance.

3.2 What is the position of the following expressed as a bearing and range:

   a) Yellow buoy marking Bournemouth Rocks from Bournemouth Pier?
   b) Fl Y 2s DZ 'A' buoy from Chapel on St Alban's Head?
   c) The entrance to Lulworth Cove from Fl Y 5s buoy?
   d) 'C' Head breakwater light Oc G 10s from a position 50° 36'.0N 2° 24'.4W?
   e) The anchorage at Chesil Cove from Fl Y 10s buoy west of Portland?

3.3 What is the true bearing of the transit of the beacons marking the eastern end of the measured distance of Anvil Point? What use could be made of this transit?

3.4 A boat is 2.0M east of St Alban's Head. Give the latitude and longitude of her position.

3.5 What is the general direction into Poole Harbour along the Swash Channel?

3.6 a) Towards which direction in three figure notation is a southeast wind blowing?
   b) In what direction is a westerly tidal stream setting?

3.7 Plot a position 2.0M southeast of the groyne at Hengistbury Head. When might you give your position in this manner? What is the latitude and longitude of this position?

3.8 At night there is a directional light at South Haven Point for the inshore entrance to Poole. What would be the true course of a boat entering Poole via the inshore entrance following the white sector of the light?

3.9 What pilotage aid is given for the entrance to Weymouth Harbour?

3.10 What use could be made of the two towers east-northeast of White Nothe (50° 37'.8N 2° 18'.3W)?

4

4 • Variation and Deviation

Use chart 15 and the deviation table in Fig 4.1

Compass Heading	Deviation
000°	4½°W
020°	4°W
040°	3°W
060°	0°
080°	2°E
100°	3°E
120°	4°E
140°	4½°E
160°	5°E
180°	5°E
200°	4½°E
220°	3½°E
240°	0°
260°	2½°W
280°	3½°W
300°	4°W
320°	5°W
340°	5°W

Fig 4.1 Deviation table

4.1 Look at the compass rose in Poole Bay. What is the variation for the year 2001? Is the variation the same on the compass rose in the approaches to Weymouth and Portland?

4.2 Complete the following table:

Compass	Deviation	Magnetic	Variation	True
	5°E	027°	6°W	
225°	2°W		2°W	
135°	4°W			134°
230°		229°		225°
358°	5°E		5°E	

4.3 To check the deviation of the steering compass, a boat is steering along a transit line using two beacons on the shore. The steering compass reads 026°C, from the chart the transit bears 030°T, variation is 3°W. What is the deviation?

4.4 A boat on a heading of 120ºC takes the following bearings using the steering compass:

Priory	345ºC
Church spire	260ºC
Lighthouse	126ºC

Variation 3ºW. Use Fig 4.1 (page 5). What are the true bearings? What is the compass error for the boat's heading?

4.5 Why is it not possible to provide a deviation table for the hand-bearing compass?

4.6 You have just purchased a boat and wish to install a new steering compass. What considerations will you take into account for siting it? What would you do after siting is complete?

4.7 Convert the following true courses to compass courses:

True	Variation	Magnetic	Deviation	Compass
016°	4°W		3°E	
003°	6°E		1°W	
185°	2°E		Nil	
356°	10°W		4°E	
085°	4°E		6°E	

4.8 What is the deviation for the following compass courses: 144ºC, 242ºC, 230ºC, 330ºC, 062ºC?

4.9 Once a deviation table has been tabulated, is it valid for the life of the boat?

4.10 Convert the following magnetic bearings to true bearings:

Magnetic	Variation	True
165°	6°W	
247°	4°E	
310°	7°E	
085°	8°W	
001°	2°W	

5 • Tidal Streams

Use Extract S

5.1 In which publications can you find details of the directions and rates of tidal streams? What use can you make of the tabulated data?

5.2 Refer to tidal stream diagram, Extract S. A boat is planning to leave Poole Harbour on passage to Weymouth. High Water, Dover, is at 1600 BST. Between what hours is there a favourable tidal stream?

5.3 What is the direction and rate of the tidal stream west of Portland Bill at High Water, Portland, at spring tides? Use Extract S.

5.4 High Water, Plymouth, is at 1030 BST. South of St Alban's Ledge, when does the tidal stream change from east-going to west-going?

5.5 Why do you sometimes experience stronger tidal streams than those tabulated?

5.6 At 1800 you are at anchor in windless conditions in Studland Bay. Your bows are pointing due north and you estimate there is a tidal stream of 0.3k. High Water, Portsmouth, is at 2355 BST and it is a spring tide. Why does the tidal stream in the anchorage appear to differ from that tabulated in tidal diamond H?

5.7 To the east of St Alban's Ledge the chart shows *Overfalls on the east-going stream*. What conditions might you expect with a strong easterly wind?

5.8 What is the direction and spring rate of the tidal stream east of St Alban's Ledge three hours before High Water, Plymouth?

5.9 What is the direction and neap rate of the tidal stream in position 50° 34'.2N 2° 15'.9W, six hours after High Water, Plymouth?

5.10 High Water, Plymouth, is at 1200 BST, springs. At 1230 BST a boat is in position 50° 30'.0N 2° 15'.0W heading towards Swanage at a speed of 6.0k. What tidal streams might she expect during the next two hours?

6 • Tidal Times and Heights

Use extracts as necessary and tidal curve graphs

6.1 Where would you find information about times and heights of tides?

6.2 a) What are the times and heights of tides on 18 June at Dover?
b) Is it a spring or a neap tide?

6.3 What is the height above chart datum of the white light at Portland Bill?

6.4 a) A boat with a draught of 1.0m requires to cross a sandbar which dries
1.1m with a clearance of 0.5m. What height of tide will she need?
b) Why is it sensible to allow a clearance?

6.5 What is the height of tide at Dover on 18 May at 0720 BST?

6.6 At what time will the tide first reach a height of 3.0m at Ramsgate on 3 July?

6.7 What is the height of tide at Folkestone on 8 August at 2000 BST?

6.8 What will be the height of tide at Lymington at 1220 BST on 17 June?

6.9 At what time will the tide reach a height of 1.9m at Yarmouth on 2 August?

6.10 In Portland Harbour on 11 July a boat goes aground at 1220 BST. At what time will she refloat?

7 • Weather

7.1 What are the following?

a) a col
b) a trough
c) a ridge of high pressure

7.2 What causes fog?

7.3 Where and at what time of the day would you expect to encounter a sea breeze?

7.4 a) What sea conditions would you expect with a wind E7 (easterly force 7) and a tidal stream setting 090ºT 3.0k?
b) How might these conditions change if the tidal stream was 270ºT 3.0k?

7.5 What information is contained in the shipping forecast?

7.6 What weather information may be broadcast by the Coastguard?

7.7 What are the services provided by MetWEB?

7.8 Concerning the movement of pressure systems, what is meant by the following terms:
a) slowly
b) steadily
c) rapidly

7.9 Under the Beaufort Scale, give the approximate wind speeds, sea conditions and wave heights for the following winds:
a) force 4
b) force 7
c) force 9

7.10 Study the surface analysis chart in Fig 7.1. If the low pressure over Malin is moving slowly eastwards, what weather might a boat expect over the next 24 hours in positions **a**, **b** and **c**?

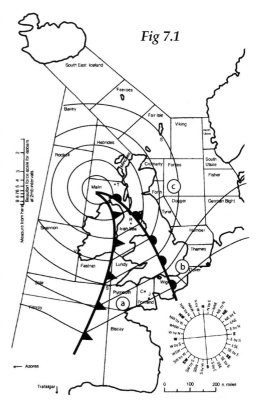

Fig 7.1

8 • Estimated Position

Use variation 3°W and deviation table Fig 4.1 (page 5). All times BST

8.1 A boat is passing the East Ship Channel entrance to Portland Inner Harbour. At 0830 (log 1.0) she is in a position 074°T from Fort Head 0.5M and sets a course of 072°M at a speed of 3.0k. Use tidal diamond A. HW Plymouth 0800, neaps. There is no leeway. What is her Estimated Position (EP) at 0930 and what should the log reading be?

8.2 A boat is approaching Portland Harbour from the southeast. At 1200 (log 17.1) her position by Global Positioning System (GPS) is 50° 34'.0N 2° 20'.0W. She steers a course of 306°M at a boat speed of 4.0k. Using tidal diamond D. HW Plymouth 1515, springs, plot the EP at 1230. There is no leeway. What is the latitude and longitude of this position?

8.3 A boat sets off at a speed of 3.0k from Weymouth Harbour heading along the Dorset coast in an easterly direction. At 1025 (log 3.8) her position is 090°T from Weymouth Harbour breakwater head 1.2M. She sets a course of 076°M. There is a northerly wind and she estimates that the leeway is 5°. Use tidal diamond A. HW Plymouth 1555, springs. Plot her EP at 1125. What is the latitude and longitude of this position?

8.4 At 0945 a boat is in position 50° 35'.1N 2° 19'.7W steering a course of 070°M towards Worbarrow Bay at a speed of 4.0k. Leeway is 5° due to a northerly wind. Plot the EP at 1045. Use tidal diamond D. HW Plymouth 1015, springs. What is the latitude and longitude of this position? If the boat continues at the same course and speed when will she reach the anchorage to the east of Worbarrow Bay?

8.5 At 1340 a boat in position 50° 34'.6N 2° 06'.9W is on the port tack beating towards Weymouth against a westerly wind. The log reading is 22.5. She steers a course of 312°C. The leeway is 10°. When the log reads 25.2 she goes about onto the starboard tack steering a course of 230°C, leeway 10°. Plot the EP at 1440 when the log reads 27.3. What is the latitude and longitude of this position? Use tidal diamond E. HW Plymouth 2010, springs.

8.6 At 1755, log 11.1, a boat in position 50° 33'.5N 2° 12'.6W makes a speed of 4.2k on a course of 077°C. There is no leeway. Use tidal diamond E. HW Plymouth 1825, neaps. Plot the EP at 1855. What is the latitude and longitude of this position?

8.7 At 1630, log 18.5, a boat is in position 50°33'.0N 2° 20'.1W. She is on a port reach in a northerly wind steering a course of 073°C with a leeway of 5°. When the log reads 20.6 she sails close-hauled on a course of 027°C with a leeway of 10°. Plot the EP at 1730, log 22.1. Use tidal diamond D. HW Plymouth 1100, neaps. What is the latitude and longitude of this position?

8.8 At 1540 (log 72.5) a boat is in position 50° 31'.7N 1° 52'.6W on a course of 313°M. Noting that there was a west-going tidal stream, at 1605 (log 74.4) she alters course to 010°M to clear Durlston Head and Peveril Point. Plot the EP at 1640 (log 76.8). Use tidal diamond G. HW Plymouth 1810, springs. No leeway. What is the latitude and longitude of the 1640 EP? If she continues on the same course of 010°M at a speed of 3.0k, will she leave Peveril Ledge red buoy clear to port?

8.9 At 0700 (log 15.6) a boat in GPS position 50° 29'.2N 1° 53'.4W is beating to the west when she encounters a line squall with a wind veering sharply between west and northwest. On the port tack she steers a course of 300°M. At 0730 (log 18.0) she goes about making 242°M on the starboard tack. At 0750 (log 19.7) the wind veers and she can now steer 302°M on the starboard tack. Plot her EP at 0800 (log 20.5). What is the latitude and longitude of this position? Use tidal diamond G. HW Plymouth 0630, neaps. Leeway is 10° throughout.

8.10 At 1930 (log 47.4) a boat in GPS position 50° 30'.6N 2° 00'.4W is heading for Poole beating against a northerly wind. Her course is 310°M and she is making 10° of leeway. At 1948 (log 48.2) she tacks onto a course of 039°M, leeway 10°. At 2035 (log 50.3) she tacks onto a course of 302°M, leeway 10°. Plot her EP at 2130 (log 52.8). Use tidal diamond G. HW Plymouth 1900, neaps. What is the bearing and range from Anvil Point lighthouse of her 2130 EP?

9 • Course to Steer

Use variation 3ºW, deviation table Fig 4.1 (Page 5) and tidal diamond Z, Fig 9.1. All times BST

9.1 On 12 June at 0741 a boat is in position 50º 42'.2N 1º 43'.9W heading at 2.0k towards a position 50º 43'.3N 1º 40'.4W. What is the course to steer and the Estimated Time of Arrival (ETA)? Use tidal diamond Z. No leeway.

9.2 On 26 June at 1149 a boat is in position 50º 41'.9N 1º 44'.2W heading at 3.5k towards a position 50º 38'.3N 1º 41'.1W. What is the course to steer and the ETA? Use tidal diamond Z. No leeway.

9.3 On 20 June at 0514, log 19.8, a boat is in position 50º 40'.0N 1º 43'.5W making for a position 158ºT from the beacon at the end of the groyne off Hengistbury Head 0.4M against a northerly wind. Starting on the starboard tack, she can make a course of 324ºC. On the port tack she can make a course of 054ºC. Her speed is 4.0k. At what time and log reading should she tack and what is her ETA at the destination position? Use tidal diamond Z. No leeway.

9.4 On 5 June at 1215 a boat is in position 50º 39'.0N 1º 45'.0W making for a position 50º 42'.3N 1º 47'.0W at a speed of 4.0k. What is her course to steer and the ETA? Use tidal diamond Z. No leeway.

9.5 At 0945, log 16.1, a boat is in GPS position 50º 29'.8N 1º 56'.0W heading for a position 50º 38'.6N 1º 53'.4W just to the east of Handfast Point. Her speed is 5.0k. Use tidal diamond G, HW Plymouth is 1215, springs. Leeway is 5º due to a northwest wind. What is the compass course to steer and what is the ETA?

9.6 At 1030, log 15.2, a boat is in position 50º 34'.4N 1º 53'.0W heading for position 50º 29'.8N 1º 53'.7W. Her speed is 4.0k. There is no leeway. Use tidal diamond G. HW Plymouth 1700, springs. What is the compass course to steer and what is the ETA?

9.7 At 1615, log 37.5, a boat is in position 50º 30'.4N 2º 01'.2W heading for a position 1.0M east of Durlston Head. Her speed is 5.0k. There is 10º of leeway due to a north wind. Use tidal diamond G. HW Plymouth 1345, neaps. What is the compass course to steer and what is the ETA?

9.8 At 1430 BST, log 16.5, a boat is in position 50º 29'.7N 2º 10'.0W heading for position 50º 36'.6N 2º 19'.0W at a speed of 3.5k. What is her course to steer and ETA? HW Plymouth 1900 BST, neaps. No leeway.

9.9 At 0930 BST, log 16.4, a boat is in position 50° 35′.7N 2° 09′.0W close-hauled on the starboard tack beating against a westerly wind. Her course is 225°C and she is making a speed of 3.0k. The leeway is estimated as 10°. She estimates her course on the port tack would be 323°C. At what time and log reading should she tack in order to pass through a position 50° 34′.6N 2° 14′.8W? What will be her ETA at that position? When is her closest point of approach to the yellow buoy Fl Y 5s and at what distance will the buoy be at that time? Use tidal diamond E. HW Plymouth 1300 BST, springs.

9.10 At 1415, log 48.4, a boat is in GPS position 50° 27′.3N 2° 16′.4W heading for E Shambles buoy at a speed of 4.0k, beating against a northerly wind. Leeway is 5°. Use tidal diamond F. HW Plymouth 1315 BST, springs. What is the compass course to steer and what is the ETA at E Shambles buoy?

		Z 50°41′.9N 1°44′.6W Rate (k)	
Hours	Dir	Sp	Np
HW–6	240	0.8	0.4
HW–5	030	0.4	0.2
HW–4	065	1.2	0.5
HW–3	075	1.9	0.9
HW–2	085	2.1	1.0
HW–1	090	1.5	0.7
HW	090	0.4	0.2
HW+1	195	0.6	0.3
HW+2	200	1.2	0.6
HW+3	204	1.8	0.9
HW+4	206	2.4	1.6
HW+5	226	2.0	1.2
HW+6	240	0.8	0.4

Tidal streams referred to HW at PORTSMOUTH

Fig 9.1 Tidal diamond Z

EXERCISES

10 • Position Fixing

Use variation 3ºW. All times BST

10.1 A boat is at anchor at the north end of Weymouth Bay. Her anchor bearings are:

> White Tower 006ºM
> Right hand edge of Redcliff Point 089ºM

Plot the position. What is the latitude and longitude of this position? What is the approximate charted depth? How much anchor cable should be veered? How much would you expect the anchor bearings to alter before being concerned that the anchor is dragging?

10.2 At 1200, log 2.2, boat at the centre of Weymouth Bay takes the following bearings:

> White Tower 032ºM
> Spire 266ºM
> Clock 246ºM

Plot the position. What is the latitude and longitude of this position? Is it a good fix?

10.3 At 1400, log 3.3, boat approaching Weymouth Harbour steers down the transit of the end of the breakwater and a tower on the south bank on a course of 257ºC. At the same time she takes a bearing of a spire near the beach in Weymouth Bay at 313ºM. Plot the position. What is the latitude and longitude of this position? Is there any deviation on the steering compass?

10.4 At 1500, log 4.4, a boat proceeding from Weymouth Harbour to Portland Inner Harbour takes a bearing of 'C' Head of North Ship Channel at 194ºM at the same time as a chimney and TV mast are in transit on a bearing of 265ºM. Plot the position. What is the latitude and longitude of this position?

10.5 A boat departing from Portland Inner Harbour by North Ship Channel steers a course of 095ºC to keep the ruin of Sandsfoot Castle midway between 'C' Head and 'B' Head. What is the deviation of the steering compass?

EXERCISES

10.6 At 0630, log 20.4, a boat in DR position 50° 37'.2N 2° 24'.5W takes a bearing of the White Tower at the northern end of Weymouth Bay at 337°M. She steers a course of 093°M. At 0730, log 22.9, she takes a bearing of the chapel on the top of Burning Cliff behind Ringstead Bay at 033°M. Use tidal diamond A. HW Plymouth 1300, springs. Plot the 0730 position. What is the latitude and longitude of this position?

10.7 A boat is off Highcliffe in DR position 50° 43'.8N 1° 41'.5W. At 1420, log 23.7, she takes a bearing of Highcliffe Castle at 303°M. She continues on a course of 240°C closehauled on the starboard tack making an estimated 10° of leeway. The tidal stream is negligible. Use the deviation table in Fig 4.1. At 1440, log 25.3, she takes a further bearing of Highcliffe Castle at 024°M. Plot the 1440 position. What is the latitude and longitude of this position?

10.8 A boat is at anchor off the groynes at Boscombe. The bearing of the lift at Portman Ravine is 333°M. The depth of water is 3.0m and the height of tide is estimated as 1.0m. Plot the position. What is the latitude and longitude of this position? If she drags her anchor, what hazards are nearby?

10.9 At 1230, log 6.6, a boat is in DR position 50° 42'.5N 1° 47'.3W. She takes bearings which when corrected are:

> Southbourne Water Tower   342°T
> Christchurch Priory Tower (40)   028°T
> Coastguard Lookout   077°T

Plot the 1230 position. What is the latitude and longitude of this position? Is it a good fix? Why is it so far from the DR position?

10.10 At 1415, log 22.5, a boat in DR position 50° 40'.5N 1° 49'.6W takes a bearing of Southbourne Water Tower at 019°M. She steers a course of 085°C at a speed of 5.0k. The tidal stream is 236°T 0.7k. She is making 5° of leeway due to a northerly wind. At 1515, log 27.5, she takes a second bearing of the Water Tower at 300°M. Plot the 1515 position. What is the latitude and longitude of this position?

11 • Pilotage

Use chart 15, variation 3ºW, deviation table Fig 4.1 (page 5) and extracts as necessary. All times BST

11.1 What is the speed limit in Beaulieu River?

11.2 What hazards should you be aware of at the entrance to Beaulieu River?

11.3 At Lymington, what is the minimum depth:

a) In the middle of the channel between the entrance and the railway pier?
b) In the middle of the channel from the railway pier to the town quay?

11.4 What are the dangers when entering Yarmouth Harbour?

11.5 At Portland Inner Harbour:

a) What are the requirements for entering and using the harbour?
b) Is it a sheltered harbour?

11.6 When approaching Anvil Point light:

a) At what distance would you expect to see it?
b) What is its arc of visibility?

11.7 At night a boat is in position 50º 34'.7N 2º 20'.9W:

a) Can she see the light at Portland Bill?
b) If so, what sequence would she see?

11.8 a) What is the bearing of the two church spires in transit at Swanage?
b) What use can be made of a transit?

11.9 You have anchored in Studland Bay. How can you check whether the anchor is dragging?

11.10 It is 17 July and your boat, which has a draught of 1.6m, is berthed in Lymington at the Town Quay. The next day you would like to go across to Yarmouth to pick up a friend, then pick up a visitors' mooring in Newtown River for lunch, and, finally, proceed to Bucklers Hard Yacht Harbour in Beaulieu River for the night. The weather forecast is fair with winds light northwesterly. Under power you can maintain a passage speed of 4.0k. Prepare a pilotage plan for the passage.

12 • Passage Plan

Use chart 15, variation 3ºW, deviation table Fig 4.1 (page 5) and extracts as necessary. All times BST

12.1 a) A boat, anchored in Studland Bay, is planning a passage westward towards Weymouth. HW Dover is at 1130 BST. At what time does she need to weigh anchor to gain maximum use of the west-going tidal stream?

b) How many hours of favourable tidal stream would she expect?

12.2 A boat, in position 000ºT from DZ 'A' buoy 1.0M, is on passage to Portland. She wishes to anchor overnight. There is a west-going tidal stream and a light northeast wind. Within 10M, what suitable anchorages are accessible?

12.3 A boat is planning to visit Yarmouth.

a) What are the daymarks for entrance to the harbour?
b) What lights are there at night?
c) Are there any hazards?
d) How would she know if the harbour is full?
e) What additional signal is shown in fog?

12.4 You have sailed from Poole intending to berth overnight in Yarmouth. As you approach you see a red flag flying from the pierhead. What does this mean? What action will you take? Give reasons. What could you have done beforehand? The wind is north force 5, there are 2 hours of east-going tidal stream remaining, and your boat draws 2.0m.

12.5 On the morning of 25 June a boat is at anchor at Chesil Cove on the west coast of the Isle of Portland waiting to make a passage round Portland Bill to Weymouth. HW at Portland is at 0754 and 2016 BST and at Plymouth HW is at 0649 and 1908 BST. There are spring tides. The wind is west force 3. Make a passage plan with the earliest and latest times of departure. Assume a passage speed of 4.0k.

12.6 On 12 June a boat is at anchor at the southern end of Weymouth Bay waiting to sail westwards to Salcombe in Devon. The wind is northwesterly force 2. Assuming a passage speed of 4.0k, between what times in the morning should she plan to sail to pass westward via the inshore passage south of the Bill of Portland? Portland HW at 0835 and 2049 and at Plymouth HW is at 0734 and 1949, springs.

12.7 On approaching Weymouth Harbour 2 red lights over 1 green light are visible from a red and white mast near the root of the south pier. What do they signify?

12.8 You are cruising in the Weymouth and Portland area and you are running low on diesel fuel and fresh water. Where can you obtain supplies?

12.9 In what weather conditions would you be ill-advised to anchor in Swanage Bay?

12.10 Your boat, draught 1.2m, is moored in Weymouth marina. HW Dover 1900, neaps. HW Portsmouth 1921 BST, neaps. Tomorrow you want to make a passage to Christchurch. The weather forecast is fair with southwest winds force 3 to 4. You expect to be able to maintain a passage speed of 5.0k. Make a passage plan.

Test Paper A

Use chart 15, chartlet 1 Weymouth and Portland. Variation 3ºW. All times BST

A1 At 1430, log 17.3, a boat has sailed from Weymouth and takes the following bearings:

> Chimney in front of White Building 076ºM
> Old High lighthouse   104ºM
> Portland Bill lighthouse   131ºT

Plot the fix at 1430. What is its latitude and longitude?

A2 At 0600 on 4 July a boat fixes her position by GPS at 50º 32'.4N 2º 20'.9W. The boat speed is 3.0k.

a) What is the magnetic course to steer for West Shambles West cardinal buoy? Use tidal diamond B.
b) What is her ETA at the buoy?
c) If there is a strong wind from the west and the leeway is estimated as 5º what course should be steered?

A3 At 1600, log 12.2, on 19 June a boat is in position 215ºT Portland Bill lighthouse 2.0M on a course of 043ºM. At 1700 the log reads 15.6.

a) Using tidal diamond C, plot the EP at 1700.
b) What is the speed made good?
c) What is the charted depth at 1700?

A4 At 1210 on 26 July a boat with a draught of 1.3m is preparing to anchor in Weymouth Bay.

a) What is the height of tide at 1210?
b) How much will the tide fall between 1210 and low water?
c) In what depth of water should the boat anchor to give a clearance of 0.5m at low water?
d) What is the quality of the bottom?

Test Paper B

Use chart 15, and deviation 3ºW. All times BST

B1 At 1050 (log 11.1) a boat is in position 50º 33'.2N 1º 53'.5W steering a course of 240ºT at a speed 5.0k. Plot the Estimated Position (EP) at 1150. Use tidal diamond G. HW Plymouth 0820, neaps. What is the latitude and longitude of the 1150 position? What is the course and speed made good?

B2 At 1220 (log 4.8) a boat is in DR position 50º 31'.4N 2º 02'.6W. The visibility is not good but she suddenly spots a light flashing every ten seconds on a bearing of 036ºT. She proceeds on a course of 052ºT then at 1320 (log 8.8) she takes a second bearing of 303ºT. Plot the position at 1320. Use tidal diamond G. HW Plymouth 1150, neaps. What is the latitude and longitude of the position at 1320? Is this an accurate position?

B3 At 1500 (log 6.3) a boat is in position 50º 37'.0N 1º 53'.4W making a speed of 4.0k. Using tidal diamond G, HW Plymouth 2115, springs, what is the course to steer to a position 0.5M south of Anvil Point lighthouse and what is the ETA at this position? Are there any hazards along the track?

B4 At 1025 on 27 May a boat anchors in Lulworth Cove in a depth of water of 2.8m. Her draught is 1.3m.

a) At what time is LW?
b) What will be the clearance beneath her keel at LW?
c) What is the quality of the bottom?

Test Paper C

C1 List the international distress signals suitable for small craft.

C2 You are on the yacht *Bluejay*. The boat is holed and sinking rapidly. What VHF message would you send? Give an example. The boat is 2.0M east of Portland Bill. There are four persons on board.

C3 In the diagrams of Fig TPC1, if a risk of collision exists which vessel must give way and what action should she take?

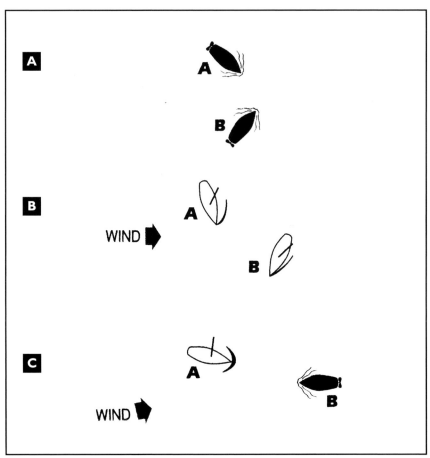

Fig TPC1

C4 In the diagrams of Fig TPC2, what is the type of vessel indicated, is she under way and what aspect is she showing?

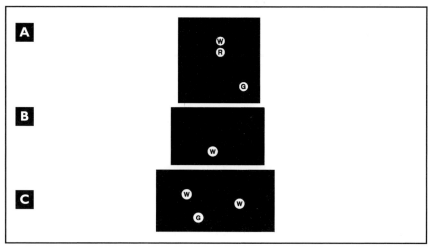

Fig TPC2

C5 What is the best type of rope for:

a) Mooring
b) Halyards
c) Dan buoy

C6 What is a good all-purpose knot? Give reasons and examples of use.

C7 Discuss the advantages and disadvantages of the following anchors:

a) Danforth
b) Bruce
c) Fisherman's
d) CQR

C8 What day shape should be shown by a vessel under sail and power?

C9 What precautions should be used when using a dinghy?

C10 You have broadcast a distress alert and a helicopter is on its way to your position. What actions could you take prior to its arrival?

C11 Which are the preferred pyrotechnics to have onboard for each of the following situations:

a) Inshore less than 3M from land
b) In coastal waters up to 7M from land
c) Offshore more than 7M from land

C12 When can water be used to extinguish a fire?

Test Paper D

D1 What lights should be shown by a yacht under sail and power?

D2 When is it not necessary to keep a lookout?

D3 For vessels within sight of each other give the correct sound signal for:

a) I wish to pass you on your starboard side.
b) You may pass on the side requested.
c) I am uncertain of your intentions.
d) I am altering course to port.

D4 Give the meaning of the following sound signals in restricted visibility:

a) One prolonged blast at intervals not exceeding 2 minutes.
b) One prolonged blast followed by two short blasts.
c) Four short blasts.
d) Two prolonged blasts at intervals of not more than two minutes.

D5 What shapes/lights should be displayed by a vessel less than 50m in length at anchor?

D6 You are berthing alongside a floating pontoon in a busy river. What mooring lines would you use? Explain the purpose of each type of line.

D7 Your anchor cable consists half of chain and half of rope. What type of rope would you use and how would you attach it to the chain?

D8 What is the principal use of the following knots:

a) Sheet bend
b) Clove hitch
c) Fisherman's bend

D9 What is the correct first aid for a person rescued from the sea who is not breathing?

D10 How would you launch a liferaft?

D11 On what occasions would you consider laying a second anchor?

D12 You wish to anchor overnight in a sheltered bay. What considerations would you take into account?

1 • *Chart Familiarisation*

1.1 The portions from chart 15 provided cover: St Alban's Ledge, Poole Bay, Weymouth and Portland. The full chart also includes Poole Harbour, Wareham Channel and Christchurch Harbour.

1.2 The scale of chartlet 1 is 1:39,000 whereas for chartlet 2 it is 1:70,000. Chartlet 1 is a much larger scale than chartlet 2 and will include more detail. (Care must be taken when transferring a position from one chart to another with a different scale. Remember to use the correct latitude and longitude scales for the chart concerned.)

1.3 Mercator projection. You should always use the latitude scale level with the boat's position as distortion occurs due to the process of projection. As latitude increases the distance representing one minute of latitude (hence one nautical mile) increases.

1.4 Cautions are warnings of specific navigational requirements or hazards. They are printed on the chart where they will not interfere with navigation. They should always be read before the chart is used.

1.5 They refer to the quality of the sea bottom: broken shells, rock and weed; soft mud and fine sand; gravel, coarse sand, pebbles and broken shells.

1.6 a) E Shambles bell buoy
b) Chapel on St Alban's Head
c) Anchorage in Studland Bay

1.7 It is a tidal diamond keyed to hourly directions and rates of the tidal stream for a particular area on the chart.

1.8 a) Plymouth
b) Portsmouth

1.9 It indicates some type of obstruction on the sea bottom so you would not anchor in this area.

1.10 It indicates that a larger scale chart is available.

2 • Buoys and Lights

2.1 Spherical yellow buoy, unlit; temporary special mark laid between April and December. It is a non-navigational buoy marking a bathing area (see caution).

2.2 No. It is obscured north of a bearing of 057°T.

2.3 1) South cardinal
2) Port hand
3) Starboard hand
4) West cardinal
5) Isolated danger

2.4 By the disposition of the colour: an East cardinal is black with a horizontal yellow band. An East cardinal buoy marks the eastern extremity of a hazard, ie the safe water is to the *east* of it, so it should be left to port on a northerly course.

2.5 Occulting green every 10 seconds, 11 metres high with a nominal range of 5 miles.

2.6 a) Canoe or spar shaped buoy or beacon with horizontal black and red bands. Topmark: two spheres vertically disposed. Light: Gp Fl (2).
b) Yes. A beacon marks an obstruction off the training bank.

2.7 A light that has different coloured sectors to indicate special navigational problems or safe passage; the white sector shows where the channel is, so if you stray too far to port you see red, and if you stray to starboard the green sector shows. Charts and pilot books give details.

2.8 **Occulting:** the light period exceeds the dark period.
Flashing: the dark period exceeds the light period.
Isophase: the dark and light periods are the same length.

2.9 To starboard. Conical, pillar or spar, green, light green, topmark conical. The symbol for the direction of buoyage is shown on the chart by an arrow between two small circles. See the example on the chart west of Swanage.

2.10 In a yachtsman's nautical almanac, or in sailing directions or in the Admiralty List of Lights. For example, Anvil Point lighthouse is described as a white circular tower.

3 • Position and Direction

3.1 a) 50º 33'.3N 2º 06'.4W
b) 50º 29'.8N 2º 24'.4W
c) 50º 33'.5N 2º 27'.3W
d) 50º 36'.3N 2º 26'.2W
e) 50º 39'.7N 1º 54'.9W

3.2 a) 228ºT 0.8M
b) 232ºT 2.4M
c) 314ºT 2.9M
d) 257ºT 1.0M
e) 117ºT 1.1M

3.3 354ºT. It could be used to check the steering compass or as a position line.

3.4 50º 34'.6N 2º 02'.0W.

3.5 334ºT, changing to 315ºT.

3.6 a) 315ºT
b) 270ºT

3.7 When sending a distress call, also in electronic position indicating systems to show the bearing and range of the next waypoint. 50º 41'.2N 2º 42'.8W.

3.8 235ºT.

3.9 A bearing of 239.6ºT of fixed red leading lights.

3.10 They could be used as a transit to check the steering compass or as a position line.

4 • Variation and Deviation

4.1 3º 35'W – (5 x 9') = 2º 50'W; though in practice we would use 3ºW. No – in the approaches to Weymouth and Portland the variation for 2001 is 3º 40'W.

4.2 022ºC, 021ºT
223ºM, 221ºT
131ºM, 3ºE
1ºW, 4ºW
003ºM, 008ºT

4.3 7ºE.

4.4 Heading 120ºC, deviation 4ºE, variation 3ºW, compass error 1ºE.
Priory   346ºT
Church spire   261ºT
Lighthouse   127ºT

4.5 The handbearing compass is not used each time from the same position in the boat. It should be held well away from any deflecting influences (rigging, engine etc) so that there will be no deviation.

4.6 A steering compass should be sited: well away from ferrous metal, magnets and electronic equipment; where the lubber line aligns with the fore and aft line of the boat. When installed in its permanent position, a compass swing should be carried out and a deviation table should be made. It is advisable to engage the services of a compass adjuster.

4.7 020ºM, 017ºC
357ºM, 358ºC
183ºM, 183ºC
006ºM, 002ºC
081ºM, 075ºC

4.8 5ºE, Nil, 2ºE, 5ºW, Nil.

4.9 No. The steering compass should be swung on every occasion that a major modification is made, like a new engine or installation of new electronic equipment.

4.10 159ºT, 251ºT, 317ºT, 077ºT, 359ºT.

5 • Tidal Streams

5.1 Tidal stream directions and rates are tabulated on the chart referred to High Water at a standard port. They are keyed in to tidal diamonds on the chart. A tidal stream atlas published by the UK Hydrographic Office or by private firms such as Reeds, or tidal stream diagrams found on some charts and in yachtsman's almanacs, show the same information in pictorial form.

The tabulated tidal stream data are used when plotting vectors on the chart as they give a more precise indication of the direction and rate than tidal stream atlases or diagrams. The tidal stream atlases and diagrams are useful when planning a passage because they show tidal direction at a glance.

5.2 From HW Dover to HW+5: 1600 to 2100.

5.3 HW Portland = approximately HW Dover –4h 30mins. 125ºT 1.5k.

5.4 At tidal diamond F the tidal stream changes from east-going to west-going at about HW Plymouth +5h 20mins. 1550 BST.

5.5 The tidal stream data show an average rate which can vary especially at spring tides and after several days of strong winds from a steady direction.

5.6 In a sheltered bay there are much weaker tidal streams and, as in this case, back eddies contrary to the main stream.

5.7 When a strong wind is blowing in the opposite direction to a tidal stream, especially flowing at spring rates, there could be a very rough and dangerous sea.

5.8 This area is tidal diamond G. 257ºT 2.4k.

5.9 This position is between tidal diamonds D and E so it is necessary to interpolate. HW–6 at D is 264ºT 1.0k and at E it is 280ºT 0.7k. By interpolation the tidal stream is 272ºT 0.9k.

5.10 At tidal diamond F at 1300 BST (HW+1) tidal stream is 068ºT 2.6k. At tidal diamond G at 1400 BST (HW+2) tidal stream is 075º 2.6k.

6 • Tidal Times and Heights

6.1 In Admiralty tide tables or yachtsman's almanacs. Local tide tables can sometimes be obtained from harbour offices.

6.2a

HW		LW		HW	
Time	*Height*	*Time*	*Height*	*Time*	*Height*
0431 GMT	5.8	1136 GMT	1.7	1657 GMT	5.9
+0100		+0100		+0100	
0531 BST		1236 BST		1757 BST	

b It is just below a mid-tide.

6.3 Height of light   43m
Height of MHWS   2.1m
Height of light above CD 45.1m

6.4 a) Draught   1.0m
Sandbar   1.1m
Clearance   0.5m
Height of tide required 2.6m

b) Silting and scouring can occur on sandbars especially in the direction of the strongest tide so the position, height and shape of sandbars can vary.

6.5

	HW		LW		
	Time	*Height*	*Time*	*Height*	*Range*
Dover	0215 GMT	6.0	0939 GMT	1.6	4.4
	+0100		+0100		(mid-tide)
	0315 BST		1039 BST		

Interval HW+4h 00min
Height of tide 3.4m

6.6

	HW		LW		
	Time	*Height*	*Time*	*Height*	*Range*
Dover	0454 GMT	5.3	11.33 GMT	2.1	3.2
Differences	+0030	−1.3	+0015	−0.7	(neaps)
Ramsgate	0524 GMT	4.0		1.4	
	+0100				
	0624 BST				

Interval HW−3h 30min
Height of tide will reach 3.0m at 03.54 BST

A N S W E R S

6.7

	LW		HW		
	Time	*Height*	*Time*	*Height*	*Range*
Dover		1.0	2256 GMT	6.5	5.5
Differences		−0.1	−0017	+0.4	(springs)
Folkestone		0.9	2239 GMT	6.9	
add 1 hour			+0100		
Folkestone			2339 BST		

Interval HW−3h 39min
Height of tide 1.8m

6.8

	LW		HW		
	Time	*Height*	*Time*	*Height*	*Range*
Portsmouth	0911 GMT	1.2		4.3	3.1
Differences	−0020	−0.3		−1.5	(critical)
Lymington	0851 GMT	0.9		2.8	
	+0100				
	0951 BST				

Interval LW+2h 29min
Height of tide 1.6m

6.9

	LW		HW		
	Time	*Height*	*Time*	*Height*	*Range*
Portsmouth	1009 GMT	1.9		3.9	2.0
Differences	−0029	−0.3		−1.2	(neaps)
Yarmouth	0940 GMT	1.6		2.7	
	+0100				
	1040 BST				

Interval LW+2h 00min
Time 1240 BST

6.10

	HW		LW		HW		
	Time	*Height*	*Time*	*Height*	*Time*	*Height*	*Range*
Portland	0723 GMT	1.9	1215 GMT	0.2	1940 GMT	2.1	1.7
	+0100				+0100		(springs)
	0823 BST		1315 BST		2040 BST		

Aground at HW+3h 57min, height of tide 0.4m.
Refloats at HW−3h 40min: 1700

7 • Weather

7.1 a) A col is an area of intermediate pressure between two low pressure and two high pressure systems. Usually associated with light variable winds.
b) A trough is an area of low pressure between two high pressure systems. Usually associated with light winds and cloudy conditions.
c) A ridge is an area of high pressure between two low pressure systems. Associated with fair weather.

7.2 Air holds water in the form of water vapour. The higher the temperature the more water vapour is held. At a given temperature, when the air can hold no more water vapour it has reached its saturation level or dew point. If this saturated air is then cooled the water vapour condenses and mist or fog is formed. A saturated air mass can be cooled by passing over either sea or land at a lower temperature or by mixing with another colder air mass.

7.3 In calm stable conditions, a sea breeze is a local wind caused by the differential heating between the sea and the land. A sea breeze always blows onto the land and is experienced up to 3 miles from the shore. It rarely exceeds force 3.
The onshore breeze commences around midday and normally reaches a peak around 1530. By sunset it has usually died away.

7.4 a) Off headlands and over a rough seabed a wind against tidal stream can cause short steep seas which can be dangerous.
b) Off headlands and over a rough seabed a wind in the same direction as the tidal stream quite often produces turbulence but, provided there is sufficient depth of water, is not necessarily dangerous. A 3.0k tidal stream against F7 would result in a near –F8.

7.5 A general weather synopsis giving the position and rate of movement of weather systems; gale warnings; sea area forecasts; reports from coastal stations.

7.6 At regular intervals the Coastguard broadcasts local area weather forecasts and strong wind and gale warnings. On request they will repeat the forecast.

7.7 MetWEB is the UK Meteorological Office prime internet website for mariners. The site is accessed on *www.met-office.gov.uk*. Some data is free of charge but there is a subscription for short and long term forecasts. Surface analysis charts and satellite pictures are available.

ANSWERS

7.8 Movement of systems
   a) less than 15k
   b) 15k to 25k
   c) 35k to 45k

7.9 Beaufort Scale
   a) Force 4: moderate breeze 11 to 16k,
      small waves becoming larger, frequent white crests, wave height 0.9 to 1.5m.
   b) Force 7: near gale 28 to 33k,
      sea heaps up, waves break, wave height 4.0 to 6.0m.
   c) Force 9: severe gale 41 to 47k,
      high breaking waves, spray affects visibility, wave height 8.0 to 10.0m.

7.10 a) Winds southwest 5 increasing to 6 then veering to northwest 4 later; heavy showers clearing later; visibility moderate becoming good.
   b) Winds southwest 3 to 4 becoming 5 later; rain at first then drizzle; visibility moderate becoming poor.
   c) Winds southerly 3 to 4 increasing 5 to 6 later; fair, rain later; visibility good becoming moderate.

ANSWERS

7.8 Movement of systems
   a) less than 15k
   b) 15k to 25k
   c) 35k to 45k

7.9 Beaufort Scale
   a) Force 4: moderate breeze 11 to 16k,
      small waves becoming larger, frequent white crests, wave height 0.9 to 1.5m.
   b) Force 7: near gale 28 to 33k,
      sea heaps up, waves break, wave height 4.0 to 6.0m.
   c) Force 9: severe gale 41 to 47k,
      high breaking waves, spray affects visibility, wave height 8.0 to 10.0m.

7.10 a) Winds southwest 5 increasing to 6 then veering to northwest 4 later; heavy showers clearing later; visibility moderate becoming good.
   b) Winds southwest 3 to 4 becoming 5 later; rain at first then drizzle; visibility moderate becoming poor.
   c) Winds southerly 3 to 4 increasing 5 to 6 later; fair, rain later; visibility good becoming moderate.

8 • Estimated Position

See answer plots

8.1 Water track 069ºT.
Tidal stream slack.
EP at 0930: **50º 36'.3N 2º 19'.7W.**
The log reads **4.0.**

8.2 Water track 303ºT.
Tidal stream 256ºT 1.2k (in 30 minutes 256ºT 0.6M).
EP at 1230: **50º 35'.0N 2º 23'.6W.**

8.3 Water track 078ºT.
Tidal stream 235ºT 0.5k.
EP at 1125: **50º 36'.9N 2º 20'.6W.**

8.4 Water track 072ºT, distance run 4.0M.
Tidal stream 053ºT 1.0k.
EP at 1045: **50º 36'.9N 2º 12'.5W.**
Speed made good 4.9k, distance to go 0.5M, elapsed time 6 mins.
She will reach the anchorage at **1051.**

8.5 Port tack: water track 314ºT, distance run 2.7M, deviation 5ºW.
Starboard tack: water track 220ºT, distance run 2.1M, deviation 3ºE.
Tidal stream 277ºT 1.9k.
EP at 1440: **50º 35'.2N 2º 15'.0W.**

8.6 Water track 076ºT, deviation 2ºE.
Tidal stream 081ºT 0.9k.
EP at 1855: **50º 34'.6N 2º 04'.8W.**

8.7 Reach: water track 077ºT, distance run 2.1M, deviation 2ºE.
Close-hauled: water track 031ºT, distance run 1.5M, deviation 3ºW.
Tidal stream 264ºT 1.0k.
EP at 1730: **50º 34'.7N 2º 17'.1W.**

8.8 Water track 310ºT, distance run 1.9M.
Water track 007ºT, distance run 2.4M.
Tidal stream 259ºT 1.6k.
EP at 1640: **50º 34'.9N 1º 56'.7W.**
Water track 007ºT.
Tidal stream 102ºT 0.4k.
She will not clear Peveril Ledge buoy without a small alteration of course to starboard.

8.9 Water track 307ºT, distance run 2.4M.
Water track 229ºT, distance run 1.7M.
Water track 289ºT, distance run 0.8M.
Tidal stream 068ºT 1.3k.
EP at 0800: **50º 30′.3N 1º 57′.5W.**

8.10 Water track 317ºT, distance run 0.8M.
Water track 046ºT, distance run 2.1M.
Water track 309ºT, distance run 2.5M.
Tidal streams 068ºT 1.3k, 075ºT 1.3k.
EP at 2130 is at 217ºT from Anvil Point lighthouse 0.6M.

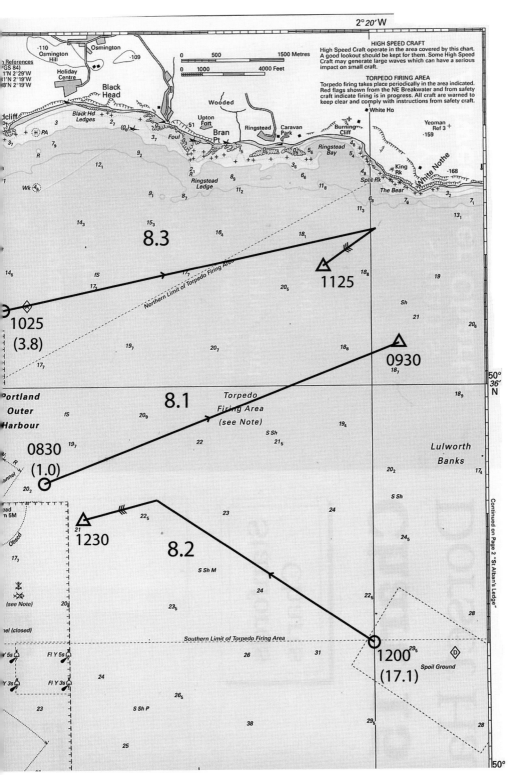

35

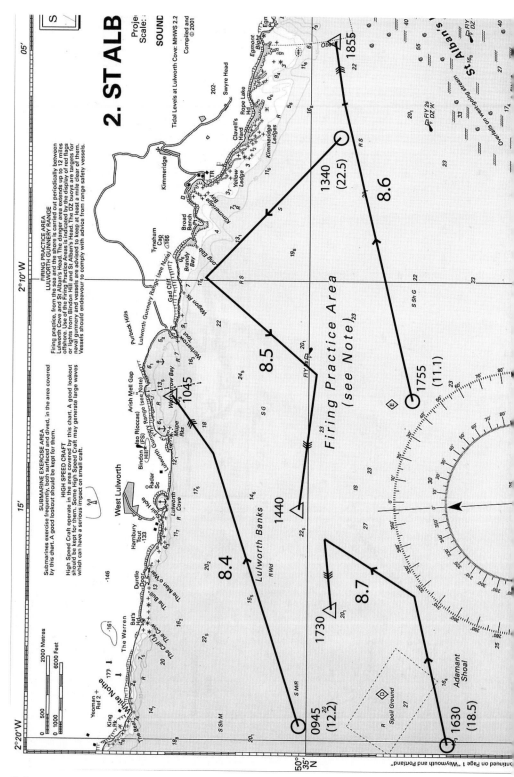

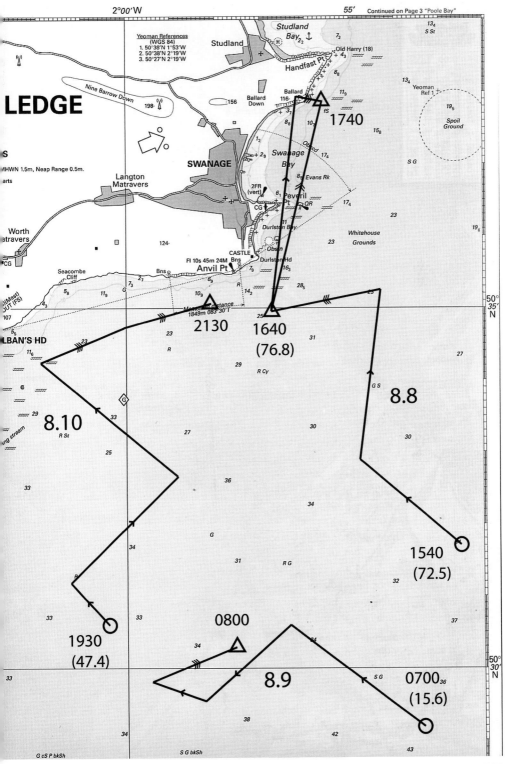

9 • Course to Steer

See answer plots

9.1 HW Portsmouth 1311, springs: tidal stream 030ºT 0.4k.
Distance to go 2.5M.
Distance made good 2.3M, speed made good 2.3k.
Elapsed time 1h 5min: ETA **0846.**
Water track 070ºT. Leeway 0º, deviation 1ºE.
Course to steer 070ºT, 073ºM or **072ºC.**

9.2 HW Portsmouth 1319, springs: tidal stream 090ºT 1.5k.
Distance to go 4.1M.
Distance made good 4.0M, speed made good 4.0k.
Elapsed time 1h 2min: ETA **1251.**
Water track 173ºT. Leeway 0º, deviation 5ºE.
Course to steer 173ºT, 176ºM or **171ºC.**

9.3 HW Portsmouth 0744, neaps: tidal stream 085ºT 1.0k.
Direct distance to go 2.4M.
Starboard tack: Deviation 5ºW, course 324ºC, 319ºM or 316ºT.
Water track 316ºT.
Ground track 328ºT, speed made good 3.4k.
Port tack: Deviation 1ºW, course 052ºC, 051ºM or 048ºT.
Water track 048ºT.
Ground track 055ºT, speed made good 4.8k.
Distance to go on starboard tack 2.3M.
Elapsed time 41 min.
Time to tack 0555, log 22.5.
Distance to go on port tack 0.6M.
Elapsed time 8 min.
ETA 0603, log reading 23.1.

9.4 HW Portsmouth 0745, neaps: tidal stream 226ºT 1.2k.
Distance to go 3.6M.
Distance made good 3.4M, speed made good 3.4k.
Elapsed time 1h 4min: ETA **1319.**
Water track 356ºT. Leeway 0º, deviation 5ºW.
Course to steer 356ºT, 359ºM or **004ºC.**

9.5 Tidal streams: 259ºT 1.6k and 102ºT 0.4k.
Distance to go 8.9M.
Distance made good 9.3M, speed made good 4.7k.
Elapsed time 1h 54min: ETA **1139.**
Water track 017ºT. Leeway 5º, deviation 4ºW.
Course to steer 012ºT, 015ºM or **019ºC.**

9.6 Tidal stream 257ºT 0.8k.
Distance to go 4.6M.
Distance made good 4.1M, speed made good 4.1k.
Elapsed time 1h 7min: ETA **1137.**
Water track 173ºT. Leeway 0º, deviation 5ºE.
Course to steer 173ºT, 176ºM or **171ºC.**

9.7 Tidal stream 079ºT 1.1k.
Distance to go 6.5M.
Distance made good 5.7M, speed made good 5.7k.
Elapsed time 1h 8min: ETA **1723.**
Water track 024ºT. Leeway 10º, deviation 4ºW.
Course to steer 014ºT, 017ºM or **021ºC.**

9.8 From 1430 to 1530 the boat is passing midway between tidal diamonds
E and F and from 1530 to 1630 midway between tidal diamonds D and
E. It is therefore necessary to interpolate the tidal streams.

1430–1530 HW–4 (neaps)	tidal diamond F	272ºT 1.7k
	tidal diamond E	278ºT 1.1k
	mean tidal stream	275ºT 1.4k
1530–1630 HW–3	tidal diamond E	279ºT 0.8k
	tidal diamond D	256ºT 0.6k
	mean tidal stream	268ºT 0.7k

Distance to go 9.0M.
Distance made good 8.3M, speed made good 4.2k.
Elapsed time 2h 9mins: **ETA 1639.**
Water track 333ºT. Leeway nil, deviation 5ºW.
Course to steer 333ºT or 336ºM or **341ºC.**

9.9 Tidal stream   0930–1030: 279ºT 1.7k
                                 1030–1130: 296ºT 0.6k

Starboard tack Deviation 3ºE, course 225ºC, 228ºM or 225ºT.
                            Leeway 10º, water track 215ºT.
                            Distance to go 3.6M.
                            Distance made good 4.1M, speed made good 4.1k.
                            Elapsed time 53 mins: **Time to tack 1023, log 19.1.**

Port tack Deviation 5ºW, course 323ºC, 318ºM or 315ºT.
Leeway 10º, water track 325ºT.
Distance to go 1.1M.
Distance made good 3.5M, speed made good 3.5k.
Elapsed time 19 mins: **ETA 1042, log 20.0.**

Closest point of approach to yellow buoy: 0.4M at 0956.

9.10 Tidal streams 1345–1445: 068ºT 2.6k
1445–1545: 071ºT 3.0k
1545–1645: 067ºT 2.8k
Distance to go 4.2M

Initial estimate of elapsed time is about one hour but, with the strong east-going tidal stream, the boat will only have travelled about 2.5M in the direction of the buoy. Use an elapsed time of 1 hour 45 mins.

Tidal streams 1415–1445: 068ºT 1.3M
1445–1545: 071ºT 3.0M
1545–1600: 067ºT 0.7M

Distance made good 3.9M, speed made good 2.2k.
Elapsed time 1h 55mins: **ETA 1610.**
Water track 282ºT. Leeway 5º, deviation 4ºW.
Course to steer 287ºT or 290ºM or **294ºC.**

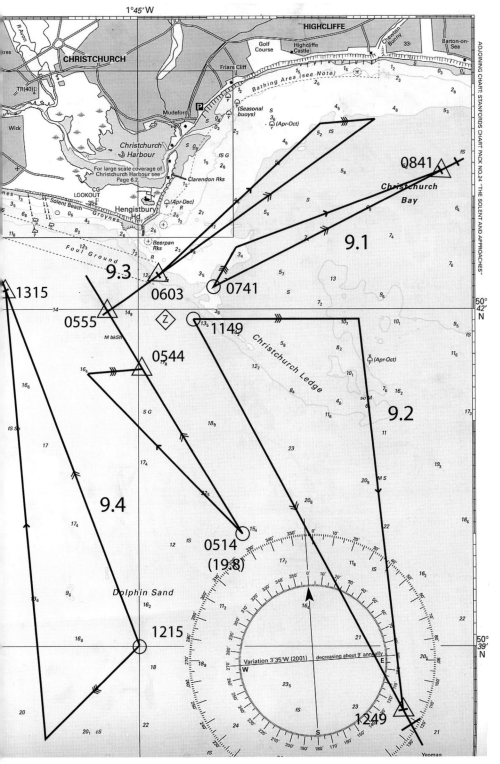

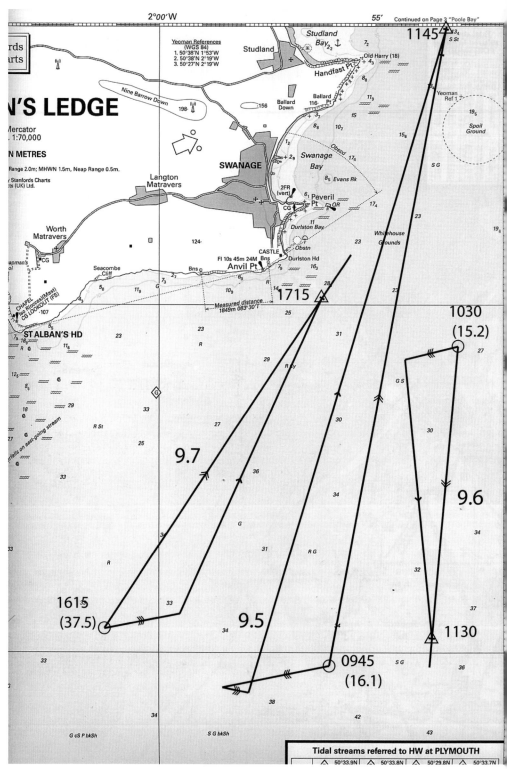

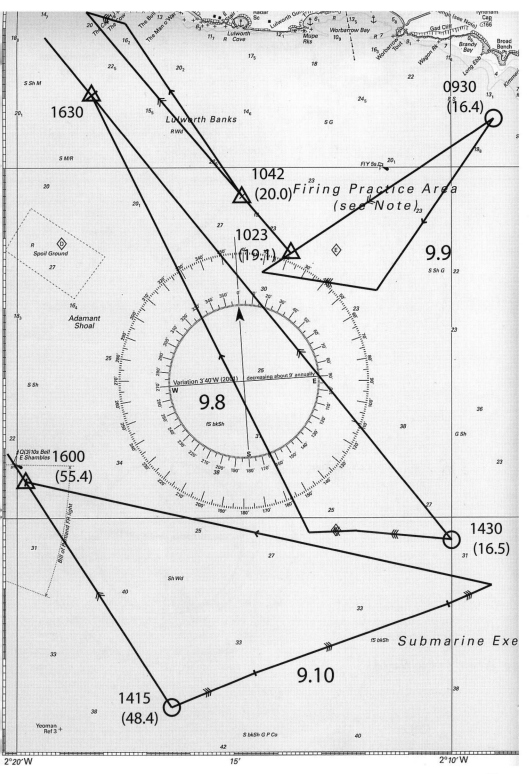

1630

0930
(16.4)

1042
(20.0)

1023
(19.1)

9.9

9.8

1600
(55.4)

1430
(16.5)

9.10

1415
(48.4)

2°20'W

15'

2°10'W

10 • Position Fixing

See answer plots

10.1 **50° 38'0N 2° 25'.1W**. Charted depth shown as 3m for which 12m of anchor cable should be veered. A difference of 5° in either anchor bearing should be treated with suspicion.

10.2 **50° 37'.2N 2° 25'.9W**. There is no cocked hat so the position can be accepted with confidence.

10.3 **50° 36'.6N 2° 26'.1W**. The true bearing of the transit is 254°T, the magnetic bearing 257°M; so there is no deviation.

10.4 **50° 36'.2N 2° 25'.8W**

10.5 True course 090°T, magnetic course 093°M, compass course 095°C: deviation **2°W**.

10.6 Water track 090°T, distance run 2.5M
Tidal stream 230°T 0.5k
Position at 0730: **50° 37'.1N 2° 21'.1W**

10.7 **50° 42'.9N 1° 43'.7W**

10.8 **50° 43'.2N 1° 48'.9W**. Close to the shore there is no tidal stream so should the anchor drag, the boat will drift downwind. Immediately to the west there is a sewer pipeline which could foul the anchor in an easterly wind. With the groynes, an onshore wind could also be dangerous.

10.9 The fix appears to be a good one but the original magnetic bearings were:

Southbourne Water Tower	339°M
Christchurch Priory Tower	025°M
Coastguard Lookout	074°M

The variation was added not subtracted so the corrected true bearings should have been:

Southbourne Water Tower	336°T
Christchurch Priory Tower	022°T
Coastguard Lookout	071°T

which gives a position **50° 42'.5N 1° 47'.4W**, close to the DR position.

10.10 **50° 40'.5N 1° 42'.7W**

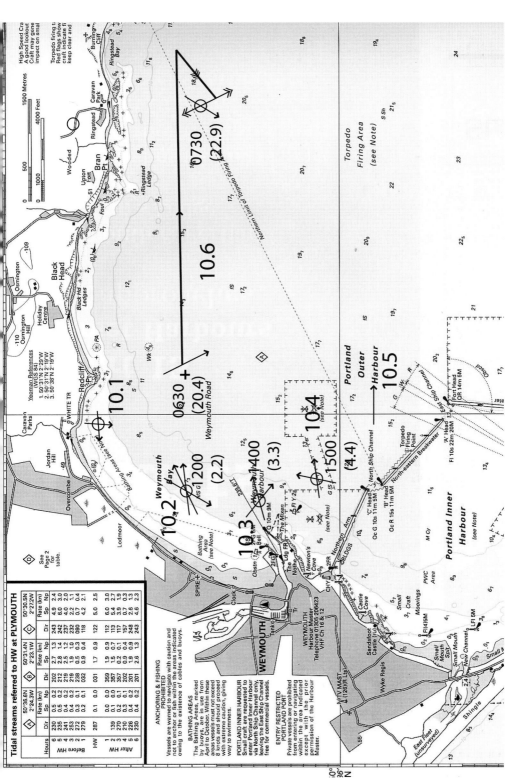

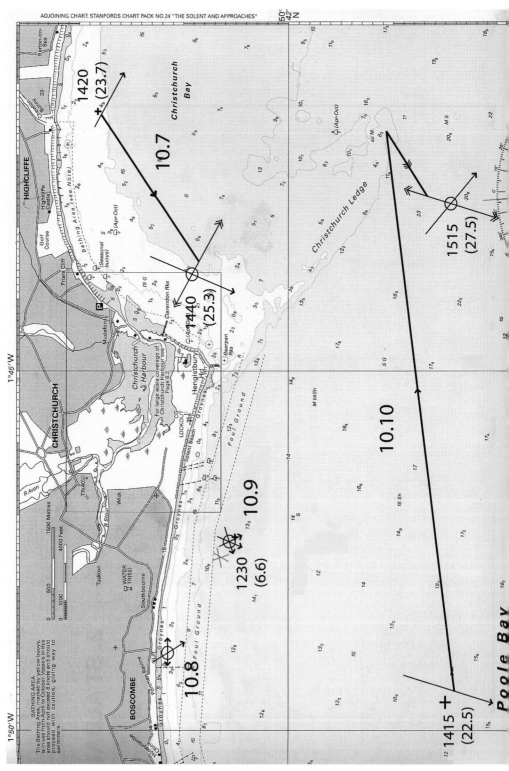

11 • Pilotage

11.1 5k

11.2 Entry is dangerous two hours either side of low water. There are patches drying 0.3m approximately 100m south of Beaulieu Spit dolphin. 200m further south-southeast, close west of the leading line, are shoal depths of 0.1m.

11.3 a) 1.8m
b) 1.1m

11.4 On the approaches: Black Rock (starboard hand mark FlG 5s), shoal water to north of E/W breakwater, ferries arriving and departing. Strong ebb stream at entrance specially at spring tides.

11.5 a) The South Ship Channel is permanently closed. Small craft are requested to enter inner harbour via North Ship Channel. The East Ship Channel is for commercial vessels. Private vessels are prohibited from entering or navigating within the area indicated off Portland Port except with harbourmaster's permission.
b) Not very sheltered due to lack of windbreaks. A better choice would be Weymouth.

11.6 a) Nominal range is 19M.
b) Obscured north of $050^\circ 37'.9^\circ$T and in the other direction north of $050^\circ 32'$T.

11.7 a) Yes.
b) Flashing (1 to 2).

11.8 a) 303°T
b) It gives a definite line of position along which the boat lies. It can be used as a clearing bearing or to check the deviation of the steering compass.

11.9 By selecting two clearing bearings as near as possible at right angles. Check these regularly. If there is no appreciable change in bearing the anchor is not dragging. Possible examples: red and white beacon ashore, end of training bank, church spire at Studland, left hand edge of Old Harry (18).

ANSWERS

11.10 Tides for 18 July:

	HW		LW		HW		
	Time	*Height*	*Time*	*Height*	*Time*	*Height*	*Range*
Portsmouth	0507GMT	4.1	1048GMT	1.3	1749GMT	4.3	3.0
	0607BST				1849BST		(mid-
Differences			−0020	−0.3			range)
Lymington			1028GMT	1.0			
			1128BST				
Differences			−0030	−0.2			
Yarmouth			1018GMT	1.1			
			1118BST				
Differences			−0020	−0.2			
Newtown			1028GMT	1.1			
			1128BST				
Differences			−0010	−0.3	−0010	−0.9	
Beaulieu (Bucklers Hard)			1038GMT	1.0	1739GMT	3.4	
			1138BST		1839BST		

Tidal streams: *east-going* HW+5 to HW−1: 1107 to 1749.
At tidal diamond E around 2 knots from 1219 to 1519
At tidal diamond F around 2½ knots from 1219 to 1519

Distances: Lymington Town Quay to Jack in the Basket 2M 30mins
Jack in the Basket to Yarmouth 2M 30mins
Yarmouth to Newtown 4M 1h
Newtown to Beaulieu Spit 4M 1h
Beaulieu Spit to Bucklers Hard 3M 45mins

Possible schedule:
Lymington Town Quay	depart	0930
Jack in the Basket		1000
Yarmouth	arrive	1030
	depart	1100
Newtown	arrive	1200
	depart	1630
Beaulieu Spit		1730
Bucklers Hard	arrive	1815

Tidal stream from 1000 to 1030 tidal diamond E (HW+4): 266°T 1.5k.
Tidal stream from 1100 to 1200 tidal diamond E (HW+5): 090°T 0.3k.
Tidal stream from 1630 to 1730 tidal diamond F (HW−2): 060°T 1.3k.

Hazards and procedures:

Lymington Town Quay to Jack in the Basket: Minimum charted depth 1.1m off Town Quay. LW height of tide at 1128 is 1.0m so minimum depth will be 2.1m. Good watch necessary for car ferries. Beware of wave screens off Lymington Yacht Haven. Channel is well marked by beacons.

Jack in the Basket to Yarmouth: The direct course is 170ºT or 173ºM. To allow for the west-going tidal stream of 1.5k it would be necessary to steer 150ºT or 153ºM. However it is more simple to steer a course into the tidal stream so as to maintain the entrance to Yarmouth harbour on a steady bearing of 173ºM. Yarmouth Harbour is dredged to a charted depth of 2.0m. Berthing on the pontoon on South Quay is permissible to pick up your extra crew member. Keep a good lookout for ferries.

Yarmouth to Newtown: The tidal stream is negligible. The course from Yarmouth pierhead to Hamstead Ledge buoy is 080ºT or 083ºM and thence 095ºT or 098ºM to the red port-hand buoy at the entrance to Newtown river. Minimum depth over the bar is 0.9m. Low water is at 1128 with a height of tide of 1.1m so the actual depth over the bar around 1200 will be 2.0m rising. From a position just west of the red port-hand buoy pick up the leading beacons (front: red and white bands with Y-shaped topmark, rear: white with white disc in black circle, on bearing of 130ºT) and thence follow the perches either towards Shalfleet Quay or to Clamerkin Lake. Visitors' moorings are white buoys. There is a public landing at Newtown Quay by black boathouse.

Newtown to Beaulieu (Bucklers Hard): From Newtown red port-hand buoy to Beaulieu Spit dolphin is 033ºT or 036ºM but the course to steer to allow for the east-going tidal stream is around 024ºT or 027ºM. After 1½ miles West Lepe port-hand buoy will be passed to port and then several yellow racing buoys. On arrival at Beaulieu Spit the height of tide will be around 2.5m. However the leading marks must be identified and the leading line of 324ºT followed from at least ½ mile southeast of the dolphin. The front leading mark is No 2 beacon, red with orange dayglow topmark consisting of a triangle above a square; the rear mark is Lepe House. Beaulieu Spit dolphin is left 40m to port. From Beaulieu Spit to Bucklers Hard the river is clearly marked by red and green beacons and perches. (Note: It makes sense to reserve a berth at Bucklers Hard Yacht Harbour the previous evening by telephone on 01590 616200.)

12 • Passage Plan

12.1 a) The distance to Weymouth is around 24M so at 4.0k the passage time would be six hours. Any favourable tidal stream would reduce this time, but it would be considerably increased if it is necessary to beat to windward. Between 1030 and 1130 the tidal stream starts to set in a westerly direction so 1130 would be the latest time to weigh anchor to benefit from a favourable tidal stream for the duration of the passage.

b) Six hours till 1730.

12.2 Worbarrow Bay and Lulworth Cove. Chapman's Pool is suitable but it is uptide of the boat's position. All these anchorages are exposed to any wind or swell from the south. They would normally be ideal as daytime anchorages in fair weather but anchoring overnight would not be advisable.

12.3 a) Daymarks: 2 white diamonds on black and white masts forming a transit on a bearing 188°T.

b) Lights: 2 leading lights FG 5/9m 2M on bearing 188°T.

c) Black Rock (starboard hand mark FlG 5s) and shoal water to north of E/W breakwater; ferries arriving and departing; strong ebbtide at entrance in spring tides.

d) A red flag is flown at pierhead and an illuminated board 'Harbour Full' is displayed at the entrance.

e) A high intensity white light is shown from the pierhead and from the inner E pier.

12.4 a) The harbour is full.

b) With a northwest wind the small craft moorings and small craft anchorage will be untenable. The best option is to go to Lymington on the remaining flood tide.

c) Radio ahead on VHF channel 68 to confirm availability of berth.

12.5 The passage information, extract U, limits the time for east-going use of the inshore passage (0.1M to 0.3M south of the Bill) from Portland HW−3 to HW+1: that is 1716 to 2116. The tidal stream diagram (extract T) shows clearly that, between these times, the tidal stream runs south-ward on the west side of the Isle of Portland and northward on the east side. The logical time to arrive at Weymouth would be at HW which is at 2016. The distance from Chesil Cove to Portland Bill is 3M and from Portland Bill to Weymouth a further 7M. Up the east coast of the Isle of Portland, the tidal streams tend to be variable but not strong so the passage time would be around 1h 45mins. So the latest time to pass Portland Bill is 1830. The earliest time is 1716. From HW−3 to HW+1

(Portland) on the west side of the Isle of Portland the tidal stream is south-going around 3.0k so from Chesil Cove to the Bill the passage time is around 30min. So the departure from Chesil Cove should be between 1645 and 1800.

12.6 The passage information, extract U, limits the time for west-going use of the inshore passage (0.1M to 0.3M south of the Bill) from Portland HW+4 to HW–6: that is 1235 to 1449. From Weymouth Bay to the Bill of Portland is 7.0M which, with the favourable tidal stream, will have a passage time of around 1h 30mins. So the time to weigh anchor would be from 1100 to 1315. Note that at HW–6 the tidal stream past Portland Bill is 6.0k which could be dangerous in a strong southwest wind. Beyond Portland Bill the tidal stream diminishes rapidly.

12.7 This is a supplementary signal to the International Port Traffic Signals. The meaning of the signal is 'Entry and departure prohibited'. Any all-round red lights shown at a harbour entrance indicate that entry and departure are prohibited but additional green or yellow lights mean that certain traffic is permitted. On VHF the Port Operations channel (Ch 12 or 14) should be monitored.

12.8 Diesel is available at Nelsons Wharf or Quayside Fuel on the south of the river just past Weymouth Sailing Club. Fresh water is available from Custom House Quay by Weymouth Sailing Club or at the Marina beyond the Town Bridge.

12.9 The anchorage is good in winds from southwest to north but bad in east or southeast winds greater than force 4, due to swell which may persist for 6 hours after a blow. In east or southeast winds greater than force 6 the anchorage is untenable and shelter should be sought in Poole Harbour.

12.10 Approximate distance is 35M which, at 5.0k, will take about 7 hours. HW Christchurch entrance is HW Portsmouth +0030 which will be 1951 and HW Christchurch Quay is 30 minutes later at 2021. Ideal arrival time would be around 1930 at Christchurch entrance. The tidal streams will be favourable throughout, though at neaps the overall speed made good is unlikely to exceed 6.0k. The passage time will be around 6 hours so a departure time from Weymouth at 1330 would seem appropriate.

It is worthwhile at this stage to plot a waypoint table.

Waypoint	Position	Lat	Long	Next waypoint Bearing	Distance
1	Weymouth marina	50° 36'.5N	2° 27'.5W	Var	0.7
2	Breakwater head	50° 36'.6N	2° 26'.4W	110°T	4.4
3	Chartlet 2	50° 35'.2N	2° 20'.0W	110°T	9.6
4	DZ 'B' buoy	50° 32'.1N	2° 06'.0W	061°T	6.0
5	0.5M south of Anvil Point	50° 35'.0N	1° 57'.5W	048°T	4.7
6	Chartlet 3	50° 38'.2N	1° 52'.0W	048°T	6.0
7	0.5M south of Hengistbury Head	50° 42'.3N	1° 44'.9W	030°T	1.5
8	Christchurch entrance	50° 43'.5N	1° 43'.8W	Var	2.2
9	Christchurch Quay	50° 43'.8N	1° 46'.4W		

Tides

	HW Time	Height	LW Time	Height	HW Time	Height	Range
Portsmouth	0536 GMT	3.7	1121GMT	1.9	1821GMT	3.9	1.8
	0636 BST		1221BST		1921BST		(neaps)
Differences					+0030	−2.4	
Christchurch entrance					1851 GMT 1951 BST	1.5	
Differences					+0100	−2.4	
Christchurch Quay					1921 GMT 2021 BST	1.5	
Portland	0006 GMT 0106 BST	1.4	0557 GMT 0657 BST	0.6	1306 GMT 1406 BST	1.3	0.8
Plymouth	2332 GMT 0032 BST	4.4	0609 GMT 0709 BST	2.0	1225 GMT 1325 BST	4.2	2.2

Tidal streams: South of St Alban's Ledge: east-going stream – Plymouth HW to HW +6: 0032 to 0632 and 1325 to 1925. Off Weymouth and Christchurch tidal streams are not significant.

Hazards: The Firing Practice Area off Lulworth and the tidal race off St Alban's Ledge would be possible hazards if close to the coast, but proposed route is well clear. On the approach to Hengistbury Head Beerpan Rocks should be avoided and also Clarendon Rocks a little further on. The entrance to Christchurch is fairly straightforward around HW and the channel is well buoyed. The only visitors' facilities are at Christchurch Sailing Club (tel 01202 483150) so it is important to reserve a berth prior to arrival.

Test Paper A

A1   50º 31′.5N 2º 28′.7W.

A2   Distance to go: 3.4M.
HW Plymouth 0032 BST, neaps. Tidal stream (HW+6): 201ºT 1.3k.
Water track: 229ºT.
Speed made good: 4.2k.
a) 232ºM.
b) Elapsed time: 49 mins. ETA 0649.
c) 237ºM.

A3   HW Plymouth 1333 BST, neaps. Tidal stream (HW+3): 117ºT 1.9k:
a) 50º 31′.0N 2º 23′.0W.
b) Course made good: 067ºT. Speed made good: 4.2k.
c) Around 28m.

A4

HW		LW		HW		
Time	**Height**	**Time**	**Height**	**Time**	**Height**	**Range**
0809 GMT	1.9	1303 GMT	0.3	2020 GMT	2.1	1.6
0909 BST		1403 BST		2120 BST		

a) From Portland tidal curves, height of tide at 1210 (HW+3): 0.9m.
b) LW at 1403. Height of tide at LW: 0.3m. Fall of tide: 0.6m.
c) Depth of water to anchor: 1.3 + 0.5 + 0.6 = 2.4m.
d) Shells, fine sand, gravel.

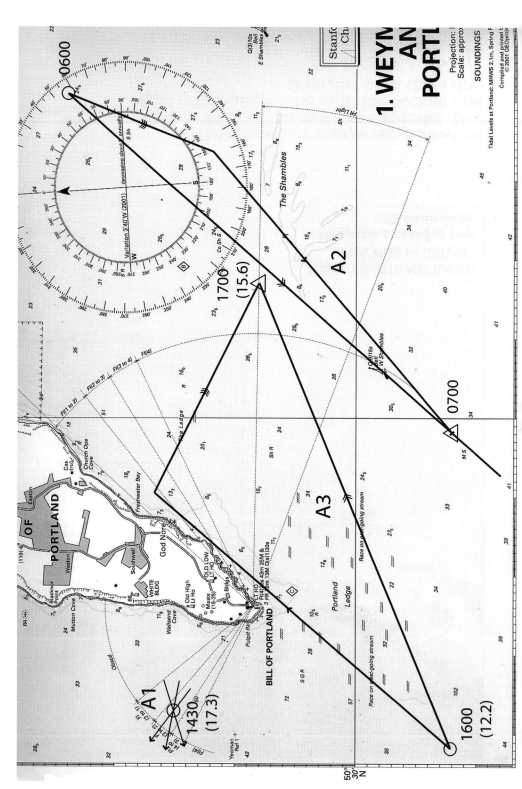

ANSWERS

Test Paper B

B1 Water track 240ºT, distance run 5.0M.
Tidal stream 079ºT 1.1k.
EP at 1150: 50º 31'.0N 1º 58'.8W.
Course made good: 236ºT.
Distance made good: 4.0M, Speed made good: 4.0k.

B2 Water track 052ºT, distance run 4.0M.
Tidal stream 068ºT 1.3k.
Fix at 1320: 50º 34'.5N 1º 55'.3W.
The accuracy depends on the correct assessment of both the boat's course and speed and the tidal stream.

B3 Distance to go 3.3M. Use ¹/₂ hour vectors.
Tidal stream 257ºT 1.6k, use 257ºT 0.8M.
Distance run 2.0M.
Water track 223ºT.
Distance made good 2.7M, speed made good 5.4k.
Elapsed time 3.3/5.4 = 37 mins.
ETA 1537.
The tidal race off Durlston Head could be a hazard particularly if a strong wind is blowing against the tidal stream.

B4

	HW		LW		
	Time	Height	Time	Height	Range
Portland	0710 GMT	2.1	1212 GMT	0.1	2.0
Differences	+0015	+0.1	–0004	+0.1	(springs)
Lulworth Cove	0725 GMT	2.2	1208 GMT	0.2	
Add 1 hour	+0100		+0100		
Lulworth Cove	0825 BST		1308 BST		

a) LW is at 1308 BST.
b) Height of tide at LW is 0.2m. From Portland tidal curves, height of tide at 1025, HW+2h 00min, is 1.6m. Fall of tide is 1.6–0.2 = 1.4m. Depth of water = 2.8–1.4 = 1.4m. Draught is 1.3m. Clearance = 1.4–1.3 = 0.1m.
c) Clay, sand and weed.

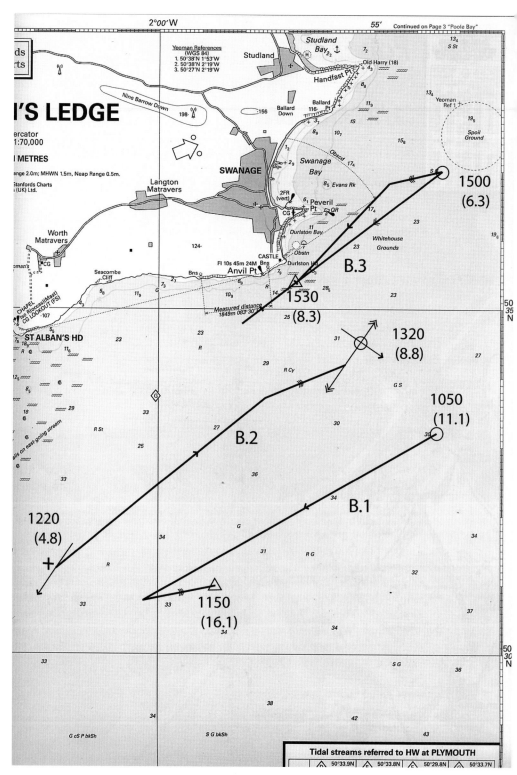

Test Paper C

C1 a) A gun or other explosive signal fired at intervals of about one minute.
b) The continuous sounding of any fog signalling apparatus.
c) Rockets throwing red stars fired one at a time at short intervals.
d) SOS (... --- ...) in Morse code by any method.
e) A signal broadcast by radiotelephony starting with the spoken word MAYDAY.
f) The International Code flag signals NC.
g) A square flag flying above or below a ball shape.
h) A rocket parachute flare or a hand flare showing a red light.
i) A signal consisting of orange coloured smoke.
j) Slow and repeated raising and lowering of arms outstretched to each side.
k) Signal transmitted by Emergency Position Indicating Radio Beacons (EPIRB).

C2 MAYDAY message
MAYDAY MAYDAY MAYDAY
This is yacht Bluejay yacht Bluejay yacht Bluejay
MAYDAY yacht Bluejay
My position is two miles east of Portland Bill
I am sinking and require immediate assistance
There are four persons on board
Over

C3 a) *Rule 15* **A** gives way as she has the other vessel on her starboard side. If she can, she should not cross ahead of **B** but alter course and pass astern, sounding the appropriate signal.
b) *Rule 12* **A** gives way as she is windward boat. She should tack or bear away and go astern of **B**.
c) *Rule 18* **B** gives way. A power driven vessel keeps out of the way of a vessel under sail. She should alter course to starboard.

C4 a) Pilot vessel, starboard side, under way and making way through the water.
b) Vessel less than 50m in length at anchor, any aspect.
c) Power driven vessel more than 50m in length under way and making way through the water, starboard side.

C5 a) A stretchable rope such as nylon.
b) Prestretched rope such as Terylene.
c) A floating line such as polypropylene.

ANSWERS

C6 A bowline. Its uses are to make a temporary eye in a rope, to join two ropes together; to attach jibsheets to sails.

C7 a) Danforth: *advantages* good holding power in sand and mud; lighter anchor needed to equal holding power of fisherman's; can be stowed flat. *Disadvantages* movable parts can become fouled; can be hard to break out of mud.
b) Bruce: *advantages* no moving parts; good holding power in sand, mud and rock; lighter anchor to give equal holding power to other types; maintains its hold if direction of horizontal pull is changed; easy to break out. *Disadvantages* difficult to stow on deck; can drag if too much cable is let out.
c) Fisherman's: *advantages* good holding power in weed and rock. *Disadvantages* awkward to stow; heavier anchor is required to give equivalent holding power to other types; anchor cable can foul the vertical fluke on seabed.
d) CQR: *advantages* holds well in sand and mud; digs in well. *Disadvantages* difficult to stow; can capsize; can drag in kelp or on hard sand; difficult to break out in mud.

C8 She shall exhibit forward a conical shape with apex downwards where it can best be seen.

C9 Wear a lifejacket; do not jump into or overload dinghy; take a torch if likely to be out at night.

C10 Put on warm clothes and don lifejackets; lower sails; stow boom down on starboard quarter; remove any running backstays; tow dinghy/liferaft astern; if any medical treatment has been given, attach label to patients explaining the details; remove dan buoys, aerials, etc from stern area.

C11 a) Red handheld flare.
b) Rocket with red parachute flare.
c) Rocket with red parachute flare.

C12 On a fire not involving liquid fuel or electricity.

Test Paper D

D1 If a sailing yacht is under power she shall show the lights of a power driven vessel less than 50m in length:
1) A white masthead light visible from ahead to two points abaft the beam on either side.
2) A red sidelight visible from dead ahead to two points abaft the beam on the port side.
3) A green sidelight visible from dead ahead to two points abaft the beam on the starboard side.
4) A white sternlight visible from astern to two points abaft the beam on either side.
(There are 32 points around a compass so each point represents an arc of $11^1/_4{}^\circ$. The arc of visibility from dead ahead to two points abaft the beam is, therefore, $90^\circ + (2 \times 11^1/_4{}^\circ) = 112^1/_2{}^\circ$.)

D2 Whilst under way at sea, a lookout by sight and sound must be kept at all times.

D3 a) Two prolonged blasts followed by one short blast.
b) Four blasts consisting of one prolonged blast, one short blast, one prolonged blast, one short blast.
c) At least five rapid short blasts.
d) Two short blasts.

D4 a) A power driven vessel making way through the water.
b) A vessel manoeuvring with difficulty, such as a vessel not under command, a vessel under sail, a vessel constrained by her draught, a vessel restricted in her ability to manoeuvre, a vessel engaged in fishing, a vessel towing or pushing another vessel.
c) Identification signal for a pilot vessel.
d) A power driven vessel under way but making no way through the water.

D5 a) A ball in the fore part of the vessel where it can best be seen.
b) An all round white light in the fore part of the vessel where it can best be seen.

D6 Head and stern lines to restrain the bows and stern; fore and aft springs to prevent the boat surging backwards and forwards; breast lines to keep the boat close to the pontoon (note that there should normally be plenty of slack in breast lines).

D7 a) A stretchable rope such as nylon. Remember that nylon is very prone to chafing so any points where chafing is likely should be protected.

b) Make an eye splice round a thimble and shackle it to the chain.

D8 a) To join two ropes together. It can be made more secure by tying a double sheet bend.

b) To attach the burgee halyard to the burgee pole.

c) To attach a warp to the anchor.

D9 Commence artificial resuscitation. If the heart has stopped apply cardiac compression. Once the patient is breathing normally and the heart is regular, place in the coma position and monitor regularly. Summon medical assistance.

D10 Do not leave the boat until it is absolutely necessary. Do not launch the liferaft until you are ready to board. Ensure that the liferaft painter is secured before it is launched. When the liferaft canister is in the water, jerk sharply on the painter to inflate the raft.

D11 a) When the boat is wind-rode in a strong wind, a second anchor laid at an angle of about 40º to the first prevents yawing.

b) To reduce the swinging circle of a boat anchored in a strong tidal stream, a second anchor is laid in the opposite direction to the first.

D12 a) Ensure that the bay is not exposed to the swell or prevailing winds both current and forecast.

b) Ensure that the holding ground is sufficient. If practical, using goggles, check that the anchor is well embedded and not foul of any obstruction.

c) Check the tide to ensure the boat will not go aground at low water and that the length of anchor cable is at least four times the maximum depth of water.

d) If there is any breeze, a boat can yaw considerably. If there are any other boats in the anchorage check to ensure that they will not hit you if they yaw during the night.

e) If there are obstructions on the seabed or if there are other yachts anchored nearby, rig an anchor buoy.

f) Note any transits or bearings as a check whether the anchor is dragging. Record the GPS latitude and longitude of the anchored position.

g) Rig anchor ball or anchor light as appropriate.

h) If going ashore, check on convenience of dinghy landing place.

i) Clear of any fairways.

j) Out of any strong tidal streams.

Extract A – Tides: Dover

TIME ZONE (UTC)
For Summer Time add ONE hour.

ENGLAND – DOVER
LAT 51°07'N   LONG 1°19'W
TIMES AND HEIGHTS OF HIGH AND LOW WATERS

MAY

Time m	Time m
1 W 0132 6.7 / 0901 0.9 / 1355 6.5 / 2114 1.1	**16** TH 0048 6.4 / 0820 1.2 / 1310 6.4 / 2038 1.3
2 TH 0217 6.3 / 0937 1.3 / 1443 6.1 / 2153 1.5	**17** F 0127 6.3 / 0856 1.4 / 1354 6.2 / 2119 1.4
3 F 0309 5.9 / 1017 1.8 / 1537 5.8 / 2241 1.7	**18** SA 0215 6.0 / 0939 1.6 / 1449 5.9 / 2208 1.7
4 SA 0408 5.5 / 1110 2.2 / 1638 5.4 / 2350 2.2	**19** SU 0320 5.7 / 1033 1.9 / 1603 5.7 / 2313 1.8
5 SU 0516 5.1 / 1227 2.4 / 1748 5.2	**20** M 0454 5.5 / 1149 2.0 / 1728 5.6
6 M 0111 2.3 / 0642 5.1 / 1344 2.4 / 1909 5.3	**21** TU 0037 1.8 / 0621 5.6 / 1317 1.9 / 1846 5.7
7 TU 0224 2.1 / 0810 5.3 / 1450 2.1 / 2018 5.6	**22** W 0153 1.6 / 0732 5.8 / 1427 1.7 / 1953 6.0
8 W 0325 1.8 / 0859 5.6 / 1546 1.8 / 2106 5.8	**23** TH 0257 1.3 / 0830 6.1 / 1529 1.4 / 2049 6.3
9 TH 0414 1.5 / 0934 5.8 / 1633 1.6 / 2143 6.1	**24** F 0400 1.0 / 0921 6.3 / 1630 1.1 / 2138 6.6
10 F 0455 1.3 / 1005 6.0 / 1712 1.4 / 2216 6.2	**25** SA 0501 0.8 / 1007 6.5 / 1726 0.9 / 2225 6.7
11 SA 0531 1.2 / 1035 6.2 / 1747 1.2 / 2246 6.3	**26** SU 0557 0.7 / 1050 6.6 / 1816 0.8 / ○2309 6.8
12 SU 0605 1.1 / 1105 6.3 / 1820 1.1 / ●2315 6.4	**27** M 0644 0.6 / 1132 6.7 / 1901 0.8 / 2352 6.8
13 M 0640 1.1 / 1134 6.3 / 1854 1.1 / 2344 6.4	**28** TU 0726 0.7 / 1213 6.7 / 1941 0.8
14 TU 0714 1.1 / 1203 6.4 / 1928 1.1	**29** W 0034 6.7 / 0805 0.9 / 1256 6.6 / 2020 1.0
15 W 0014 6.4 / 0746 1.1 / 1234 6.4 / 2002 1.1	**30** TH 0117 6.5 / 0841 1.2 / 1339 6.4 / 2058 1.2
	31 F 0201 6.2 / 0917 1.5 / 1424 6.2 / 2137 1.5

JUNE

Time m	Time m
1 SA 0249 5.9 / 0954 1.8 / 1513 5.9 / 2220 1.8	**16** SU 0218 6.1 / 0940 1.5 / 1450 6.2 / 2211 1.4
2 SU 0343 5.5 / 1037 2.0 / 1606 5.6 / 2314 2.0	**17** M 0320 5.9 / 1033 1.6 / 1551 6.0 / 2310 1.5
3 M 0442 5.3 / 1138 2.3 / 1705 5.4	**18** TU 0431 5.8 / 1136 1.7 / 1657 5.9
4 TU 0021 2.1 / 0547 5.2 / 1249 2.3 / 1811 5.4	**19** W 0015 1.5 / 0546 5.7 / 1245 1.7 / 1807 5.9
5 W 0126 2.1 / 0657 5.2 / 1353 2.2 / 1917 5.4	**20** TH 0121 1.5 / 0658 5.8 / 1351 1.7 / 1917 6.0
6 TH 0224 1.9 / 0756 5.4 / 1450 2.0 / 2011 5.6	**21** F 0225 1.4 / 0801 5.9 / 1455 1.5 / 2021 6.1
7 F 0315 1.7 / 0842 5.6 / 1541 1.8 / 2055 5.8	**22** SA 0329 1.3 / 0856 6.1 / 1600 1.4 / 2117 6.3
8 SA 0404 1.5 / 0920 5.8 / 1628 1.5 / 2132 6.0	**23** SU 0435 1.1 / 0947 6.2 / 1702 1.2 / 2209 6.4
9 SU 0449 1.5 / 0957 6.0 / 1711 1.4 / 2208 6.2	**24** M 0535 1.0 / 1035 6.4 / 1756 1.1 / ○2257 6.5
10 M 0533 1.2 / 1033 6.2 / 1753 1.2 / ●2245 6.3	**25** TU 0625 1.0 / 1119 6.5 / 1843 1.0 / 2341 6.5
11 TU 0614 1.1 / 1109 6.3 / 1833 1.1 / 2322 6.4	**26** W 0709 1.0 / 1200 6.5 / 1926 1.0
12 W 0654 1.1 / 1145 6.4 / 1912 1.1	**27** TH 0023 6.4 / 0748 1.1 / 1242 6.5 / 2006 1.1
13 TH 0000 6.4 / 0733 1.1 / 1225 6.4 / 1952 1.1	**28** F 0104 6.3 / 0825 1.3 / 1323 6.4 / 2044 1.3
14 F 0041 6.4 / 0812 1.2 / 1308 6.4 / 2034 1.1	**29** SA 0144 6.1 / 0859 1.5 / 1404 6.3 / 2120 1.4
15 SA 0126 6.3 / 0854 1.3 / 1355 6.3 / 2119 1.2	**30** SU 0226 5.7 / 0930 1.6 / 1445 6.1 / 2155 1.6

JULY

Time m	Time m
1 M 0310 5.7 / 1003 1.8 / 1528 5.9 / 2233 1.8	**16** TU 0303 6.2 / 1023 1.3 / 1529 6.4 / 2255 1.1
2 TU 0359 5.5 / 1043 2.0 / 1614 5.6 / 2319 1.9	**17** W 0401 6.0 / 1113 1.5 / 1626 6.2 / 2348 1.3
3 W 0454 5.3 / 1133 2.1 / 1708 5.5	**18** TH 0506 5.8 / 1210 1.7 / 1730 6.0
4 TH 0016 2.0 / 0554 5.2 / 1239 2.2 / 1809 5.4	**19** F 0047 1.5 / 0618 5.7 / 1315 1.8 / 1841 5.8
5 F 0120 2.0 / 0656 5.3 / 1349 2.2 / 1911 5.4	**20** SA 0152 1.6 / 0731 5.6 / 1424 1.8 / 1957 5.8
6 SA 0223 1.9 / 0752 5.4 / 1452 2.0 / 2005 5.6	**21** SU 0301 1.6 / 0837 5.7 / 1536 1.7 / 2105 5.9
7 SU 0321 1.7 / 0841 5.6 / 1549 1.8 / 2054 5.8	**22** M 0415 1.5 / 0935 6.0 / 1646 1.5 / 2204 6.1
8 M 0415 1.5 / 0926 5.9 / 1641 1.5 / 2139 6.1	**23** TU 0520 1.4 / 1025 6.2 / 1744 1.3 / 2253 6.3
9 TU 0506 1.3 / 1008 6.1 / 1729 1.3 / 2223 6.3	**24** W 0612 1.3 / 1108 6.4 / 1833 1.2 / ○2335 6.3
10 W 0554 1.2 / 1051 6.3 / 1815 1.1 / ●2307 6.4	**25** TH 0656 1.2 / 1148 6.5 / 1915 1.1
11 TH 0640 1.1 / 1133 6.5 / 1901 1.0 / 2351 6.5	**26** F 0013 6.3 / 0733 1.2 / 1227 6.5 / 1953 1.1
12 F 0725 1.1 / 1216 6.6 / 1947 0.9	**27** SA 0049 6.3 / 0807 1.3 / 1304 6.5 / 2026 1.2
13 SA 0035 6.5 / 0809 1.1 / 1301 6.6 / 2033 0.9	**28** SU 0124 6.2 / 0836 1.4 / 1340 6.4 / 2056 1.3
14 SU 0121 6.5 / 0854 1.1 / 1347 6.6 / 2119 0.9	**29** M 0158 6.0 / 0901 1.4 / 1412 6.3 / 2123 1.4
15 M 0210 6.4 / 0938 1.1 / 1436 6.5 / 2206 1.0	**30** TU 0230 5.9 / 0929 1.5 / 1442 6.1 / 2153 1.5
	31 W 0303 5.7 / 1002 1.7 / 1515 5.9 / 2229 1.7

AUGUST

Time m	Time m
1 TH 0341 5.5 / 1041 1.9 / 1558 5.6 / 2312 1.9	**16** F 0430 5.8 / 1136 1.7 / 1658 5.9
2 F 0435 5.3 / 1130 2.1 / 1657 5.4	**17** SA 0014 1.7 / 0542 5.5 / 1242 2.0 / 1812 5.6
3 SA 0011 2.1 / 0554 5.2 / 1240 2.3 / 1814 5.3	**18** SU 0123 2.0 / 0703 5.4 / 1359 2.1 / 1941 5.5
4 SU 0131 2.2 / 0709 5.2 / 1406 2.3 / 1927 5.4	**19** M 0241 2.0 / 0823 5.5 / 1524 2.0 / 2105 5.7
5 M 0245 2.0 / 0810 5.5 / 1517 2.1 / 2028 5.7	**20** TU 0407 1.8 / 0927 5.8 / 1642 1.7 / 2205 6.0
6 TU 0348 1.7 / 0903 5.8 / 1616 1.6 / 2121 6.0	**21** W 0514 1.6 / 1016 6.1 / 1738 1.4 / 2249 6.2
7 W 0444 1.4 / 0951 6.1 / 1709 1.3 / 2210 6.3	**22** TH 0602 1.4 / 1055 6.4 / 1824 1.1 / ○2325 6.3
8 TH 0537 1.2 / 1036 6.4 / 1759 1.0 / ●2256 6.5	**23** F 0642 1.3 / 1132 6.6 / 1902 1.1 / 2357 6.4
9 F 0627 1.0 / 1119 6.7 / 1850 0.8 / 2340 6.6	**24** SA 0716 1.2 / 1207 6.6 / 1934 1.1
10 SA 0716 0.9 / 1202 6.8 / 1939 0.7	**25** SU 0027 6.4 / 0743 1.3 / 1241 6.6 / 2000 1.1
11 SU 0023 6.7 / 0801 0.8 / 1246 6.9 / 2025 0.6	**26** M 0057 6.3 / 0806 1.3 / 1311 6.5 / 2024 1.2
12 M 0106 6.7 / 0843 0.8 / 1329 6.9 / 2108 0.6	**27** TU 0124 6.2 / 0828 1.3 / 1335 6.4 / 2048 1.3
13 TU 0150 6.6 / 0923 0.9 / 1415 6.7 / 2149 0.7	**28** W 0146 6.1 / 0855 1.4 / 1357 6.3 / 2116 1.4
14 W 0237 6.4 / 1002 1.1 / 1503 6.6 / 2231 1.0	**29** TH 0208 6.0 / 0926 1.5 / 1424 6.1 / 2148 1.6
15 TH 0330 6.2 / 1045 1.3 / 1556 6.3 / 2317 1.3	**30** F 0239 5.8 / 1001 1.8 / 1501 5.9 / 2225 1.9
	31 SA 0320 5.5 / 1042 2.1 / 1551 5.5 / 2312 2.2

Extract B – Tides: Portsmouth

TIME ZONE (UTC)
For Summer Time add ONE hour.

ENGLAND – PORTSMOUTH
LAT 50°48'N   LONG 1°07'W
TIMES AND HEIGHTS OF HIGH AND LOW WATERS

MAY

Day	Time	m	Time	m	Time	m	Time	m
1 W	0150	4.7	0722	0.8	1420	4.5	1941	1.1
2 TH	0230	4.4	0803	1.1	1506	4.3	2026	1.4
3 F	0313	4.1	0851	1.4	1557	4.0	2122	1.8
4 SA	0403	3.8	0953	1.7	1701	3.8	2235	2.0
5 SU	0510	3.6	1114	1.9	1825	3.8	2359	2.1
6 M	0645	3.6	1235	1.9	1942	3.9		
7 TU	0112	1.9	0802	3.7	1307	1.7	2036	4.1
8 W	0205	1.6	0853	3.9	1421	1.5	2118	4.2
9 TH	0246	1.4	0933	4.2	1501	1.2	2154	4.3
10 F	0323	1.2	1009	4.1	1538	1.1	2228	4.4
11 SA	0359	1.0	1044	4.2	1613	1.0	2301	4.4
12 SU	0433	0.9	1119	4.3	1647	0.9	● 2334	4.5
13 M	0505	0.9	1154	4.4	1719	0.9		
14 TU	0007	4.5	0536	0.9	1231	4.4	1750	1.0
15 W	0041	4.5	0607	0.9	1307	4.4	1824	1.1
16 TH	0116	4.4	0643	1.0	1346	4.4	1903	1.2
17 F	0153	4.3	0724	1.1	1429	4.3	1949	1.4
18 SA	0238	4.2	0814	1.3	1521	4.2	2046	1.6
19 SU	0334	4.0	0917	1.5	1625	4.1	2158	1.7
20 M	0441	3.9	1035	1.5	1740	4.0	2319	1.7
21 TU	0559	3.9	1156	1.5	1856	4.2		
22 W	0036	1.5	0715	4.1	1307	1.3	2000	4.4
23 TH	0140	1.3	0819	4.3	1405	1.0	2056	4.6
24 F	0235	1.0	0916	4.5	1457	0.8	2147	4.7
25 SA	0325	0.8	1009	4.6	1545	0.7	2235	4.8
26 SU	0413	0.6	1059	4.7	1631	0.6	○ 2322	4.9
27 M	0458	0.6	1147	4.7	1716	0.7		
28 TU	0006	4.8	0542	0.6	1234	4.7	1758	0.8
29 W	0048	4.7	0623	0.7	1318	4.6	1840	0.9
30 TH	0128	4.6	0704	0.8	1402	4.5	1921	1.2
31 F	0207	4.4	0744	1.1	1446	4.3	2005	1.4

JUNE

Day	Time	m	Time	m	Time	m	Time	m
1 SA	0249	4.1	0828	1.4	1533	4.1	2054	1.7
2 SU	0335	3.9	0919	1.6	1625	4.0	2152	1.9
3 M	0429	3.7	1021	1.8	1726	3.9	2301	2.0
4 TU	0534	3.6	1131	1.9	1832	3.9	2359	2.1
5 W	0012	2.0	0645	3.6	1237	1.8	1932	4.0
6 TH	0112	1.8	0749	3.7	1330	1.6	2022	4.1
7 F	0200	1.6	0841	3.9	1416	1.5	2106	4.2
8 SA	0242	1.4	0926	4.0	1457	1.3	2147	4.3
9 SU	0322	1.2	1009	4.2	1537	1.2	2226	4.4
10 M	0400	1.1	1050	4.3	1615	1.1	● 2305	4.5
11 TU	0437	1.0	1131	4.4	1653	1.1	2343	4.5
12 W	0515	0.9	1211	4.5	1733	1.0		
13 TH	0022	4.5	0555	0.9	1253	4.5	1814	1.0
14 F	0102	4.5	0637	0.9	1337	4.5	1858	1.1
15 SA	0145	4.4	0723	1.0	1424	4.5	1947	1.2
16 SU	0233	4.3	0814	1.1	1516	4.4	2042	1.3
17 M	0326	4.2	0911	1.2	1614	4.3	2143	1.4
18 TU	0427	4.1	1013	1.3	1717	4.3	2249	1.5
19 W	0534	4.1	1120	1.3	1824	4.3	2359	1.5
20 TH	0644	4.1	1228	1.3	1929	4.4		
21 F	0107	1.3	0751	4.2	1333	1.2	2029	4.5
22 SA	0209	1.2	0854	4.3	1432	1.1	2124	4.6
23 SU	0304	1.0	0951	4.4	1524	1.0	2215	4.6
24 M	0354	0.9	1044	4.5	1613	1.0	○ 2303	4.7
25 TU	0442	0.8	1134	4.6	1659	1.0	2347	4.6
26 W	0526	0.8	1219	4.6	1742	1.0		
27 TH	0028	4.6	0608	0.8	1302	4.6	1823	1.1
28 F	0107	4.5	0647	1.0	1343	4.5	1902	1.2
29 SA	0145	4.3	0725	1.1	1423	4.4	1942	1.4
30 SU	0224	4.2	0802	1.3	1503	4.3	2023	1.5

JULY

Day	Time	m	Time	m	Time	m	Time	m
1 M	0305	4.0	0842	1.4	1546	4.1	2107	1.7
2 TU	0349	3.9	0927	1.6	1632	4.0	2158	1.9
3 W	0439	3.8	1019	1.8	1723	3.9	2258	1.9
4 TH	0536	3.7	1121	1.9	1821	3.9		
5 F	0005	1.9	0641	3.7	1228	1.8	1921	4.0
6 SA	0107	1.8	0747	3.8	1327	1.7	2018	4.1
7 SU	0200	1.6	0846	4.0	1418	1.6	2109	4.2
8 M	0247	1.4	0938	4.1	1505	1.4	2156	4.3
9 TU	0332	1.2	1026	4.3	1550	1.2	2240	4.5
10 W	0416	1.0	1111	4.5	1635	1.1	● 2323	4.5
11 TH	0500	0.8	1156	4.6	1720	1.0		
12 F	0006	4.6	0545	0.8	1241	4.6	1805	0.9
13 SA	0051	4.6	0631	0.7	1327	4.7	1852	0.9
14 SU	0136	4.6	0717	0.7	1414	4.7	1940	0.9
15 M	0224	4.5	0805	0.8	1503	4.6	2029	1.0
16 TU	0315	4.4	0855	0.9	1554	4.5	2122	1.2
17 W	0408	4.3	0948	1.1	1649	4.4	2220	1.3
18 TH	0507	4.1	1048	1.3	1749	4.3	2326	1.5
19 F	0614	4.0	1155	1.5	1856	4.2		
20 SA	0038	1.5	0727	4.0	1308	1.5	2004	4.2
21 SU	0148	1.4	0842	4.1	1414	1.5	2107	4.3
22 M	0249	1.3	0942	4.2	1512	1.3	2202	4.4
23 TU	0342	1.1	1037	4.4	1602	1.2	2250	4.5
24 W	0429	1.0	1124	4.5	1646	1.1	○ 2332	4.5
25 TH	0512	0.9	1206	4.5	1728	1.1		
26 F	0011	4.5	0550	0.9	1245	4.5	1805	1.1
27 SA	0047	4.5	0627	0.9	1321	4.5	1841	1.1
28 SU	0121	4.3	0701	1.0	1355	4.4	1916	1.2
29 M	0156	4.3	0733	1.1	1429	4.4	1949	1.3
30 TU	0233	4.2	0804	1.3	1505	4.3	2023	1.5
31 W	0311	4.0	0838	1.4	1543	4.2	2101	1.7

AUGUST

Day	Time	m	Time	m	Time	m	Time	m
1 TH	0351	3.9	0917	1.7	1624	4.0	2148	1.8
2 F	0440	3.8	1009	1.9	1716	3.9	2250	2.0
3 SA	0542	3.7	1118	2.0	1821	3.9		
4 SU	0010	2.0	0659	3.7	1240	2.0	1934	4.0
5 M	0125	1.8	0814	3.9	1349	1.8	2038	4.1
6 TU	0223	1.5	0915	4.1	1445	1.6	2132	4.3
7 W	0313	1.2	1007	4.4	1534	1.3	2219	4.5
8 TH	0400	0.9	1054	4.6	1621	1.1	● 2305	4.6
9 F	0446	0.7	1140	4.7	1707	0.9	2350	4.7
10 SA	0532	0.6	1225	4.8	1753	0.7		
11 SU	0036	4.7	0617	0.5	1311	4.8	1838	0.7
12 M	0122	4.7	0702	0.5	1357	4.8	1923	0.7
13 TU	0209	4.8	0747	0.6	1442	4.8	2009	0.8
14 W	0256	4.5	0832	0.8	1528	4.6	2057	1.0
15 TH	0345	4.4	0921	1.1	1617	4.4	2151	1.3
16 F	0440	4.1	1018	1.4	1714	4.2	2256	1.6
17 SA	0546	3.9	1129	1.7	1825	4.0		
18 SU	0016	1.7	0711	3.9	1251	1.8	1947	4.0
19 M	0136	1.7	0835	4.0	1406	1.7	2058	4.1
20 TU	0241	1.5	0939	4.2	1504	1.5	2154	4.3
21 W	0332	1.2	1029	4.4	1551	1.3	2239	4.4
22 TH	0414	1.0	1111	4.5	1632	1.2	○ 2318	4.5
23 F	0453	0.9	1149	4.5	1709	1.0	2352	4.5
24 SA	0529	0.8	1222	4.6	1744	1.0		
25 SU	0024	4.4	0602	0.8	1254	4.5	1817	1.0
26 M	0056	4.4	0633	0.9	1323	4.5	1847	1.1
27 TU	0128	4.4	0701	1.0	1354	4.4	1914	1.2
28 W	0200	4.3	0727	1.2	1425	4.4	1942	1.3
29 TH	0233	4.2	0755	1.3	1457	4.4	2015	1.5
30 F	0309	4.0	0830	1.6	1532	4.1	2055	1.7
31 SA	0351	3.9	0916	1.9	1618	3.9	2151	2.0

EXTRACTS

Extract C – Tides: Portland

TIME ZONE (UTC)
For Summer Time add ONE hour.

ENGLAND – PORTLAND
LAT 50°34′N LONG 2°26′W
TIMES AND HEIGHTS OF HIGH AND LOW WATERS

MAY

Day	Time	m	Day	Time	m
1	0208	0.2	**16**	0136	0.3
	0925	1.9		0856	1.8
	W 1427	0.3		TH 1354	0.3
	2139	1.9		2102	1.8
2	0247	0.3	**17**	0210	0.3
	0957	1.7		0928	1.6
	TH 1502	0.5		F 1429	0.4
	2208	1.7		2133	1.7
3	0329	0.5	**18**	0250	0.4
	1031	1.4		1007	1.5
	F 1539	0.7		SA 1514	0.6
	2241	1.5		2215	1.6
4	0423	0.7	**19**	0346	0.5
	1118	1.3		1103	1.4
	SA 1630	0.8		SU 1621	0.7
	2330	1.4		2314	1.6
5	0544	0.8	**20**	0506	0.6
	1236	1.2		1223	1.4
	SU 1801	0.9		M 1752	0.7
6	0050	1.4	**21**	0036	1.5
	0728	0.7		0639	0.6
	M 1448	1.3		TU 1358	1.6
	1932	0.9		1919	0.7
7	0240	1.4	**22**	0209	1.6
	0832	0.6		0759	0.5
	TU 1546	1.4		W 1515	1.6
	2036	0.8		2029	0.6
8	0342	1.5	**23**	0327	1.8
	0913	0.6		0901	0.3
	W 1628	1.6		TH 1618	1.8
	2123	0.6		2126	0.4
9	0430	1.7	**24**	0432	1.9
	0952	0.4		0954	0.2
	TH 1708	1.7		F 1713	2.0
	2206	0.5		2216	0.3
10	0515	1.8	**25**	0530	2.0
	1030	0.3		1043	0.1
	F 1746	1.9		SA 1804	2.1
	2247	0.3		2304	0.2
11	0558	1.9	**26**	0622	2.1
	1108	0.2		1129	0.1
	SA 1824	2.0		SU 1852	2.2
	2325	0.3		○ 2349	0.2
12	0639	2.0	**27**	0710	2.1
	1144	0.2		1212	0.1
	SU 1901	2.0		M 1934	2.2
	●				
13	0001	0.2	**28**	0032	0.2
	0718	2.0		0753	2.1
	M 1218	0.2		TU 1254	0.2
	1935	2.0		2013	2.2
14	0034	0.2	**29**	0113	0.2
	0754	1.9		0833	2.0
	TU 1250	0.2		W 1332	0.3
	2007	2.0		2049	2.1
15	0104	0.2	**30**	0153	0.3
	0826	1.9		0908	1.8
	W 1321	0.3		TH 1409	0.4
	2034	1.9		2120	1.9
			31	0233	0.4
				0940	1.6
				F 1445	0.5
				2148	1.7

JUNE

Day	Time	m	Day	Time	m
1	0315	0.5	**16**	0257	0.4
	1013	1.5		1015	1.7
	SA 1521	0.7		SU 1524	0.5
	2218	1.6		2223	1.8
2	0401	0.6	**17**	0351	0.4
	1054	1.3		1107	1.6
	SU 1604	0.8		M 1621	0.6
	2259	1.5		2316	1.7
3	0501	0.7	**18**	0455	0.5
	1150	1.3		1210	1.5
	M 1708	0.9		TU 1728	0.6
	2356	1.4			
4	0615	0.7	**19**	0021	1.6
	1305	1.3		0607	0.5
	TU 1832	0.9		W 1323	1.6
				1841	0.7
5	0111	1.4	**20**	0136	1.6
	0725	0.6		0720	0.5
	W 1426	1.4		TH 1437	1.6
	1943	0.8		1952	0.6
6	0227	1.4	**21**	0251	1.7
	0820	0.6		0827	0.4
	TH 1527	1.5		F 1544	1.7
	2039	0.7		2057	0.6
7	0332	1.5	**22**	0401	1.7
	0906	0.5		0928	0.4
	F 1617	1.6		SA 1644	1.9
	2127	0.6		2154	0.5
8	0428	1.6	**23**	0504	1.8
	0949	0.4		1022	0.3
	SA 1703	1.8		SU 1739	2.0
	2210	0.5		2246	0.4
9	0519	1.8	**24**	0602	1.9
	1029	0.3		1111	0.3
	SU 1748	1.9		M 1830	2.1
	2250	0.4		○ 2334	0.3
10	0607	1.8	**25**	0654	1.9
	1108	0.3		1156	0.3
	M 1831	2.0		TU 1916	2.1
	● 2329	0.3			
11	0652	1.9	**26**	0019	0.3
	1148	0.2		0740	1.9
	TU 1911	2.0		W 1239	0.3
				1957	2.1
12	0008	0.3	**27**	0102	0.3
	0735	1.9		0821	1.9
	W 1228	0.3		TH 1319	0.3
	1949	2.0		2034	2.0
13	0047	0.3	**28**	0142	0.3
	0815	1.9		0856	1.8
	TH 1309	0.3		F 1356	0.4
	2026	2.0		2105	1.9
14	0127	0.3	**29**	0221	0.3
	0853	1.8		0926	1.7
	F 1351	0.3		SA 1432	0.5
	2101	1.9		2132	1.8
15	0210	0.3	**30**	0259	0.4
	0931	1.7		0954	1.6
	SA 1435	0.4		SU 1505	0.5
	2139	1.9		2201	1.7

JULY

Day	Time	m	Day	Time	m
1	0336	0.5	**16**	0342	0.3
	1027	1.4		1057	1.7
	M 1537	0.6		TU 1605	0.4
	2233	1.6		2308	1.8
2	0413	0.5	**17**	0435	0.4
	1108	1.4		1145	1.6
	TU 1611	0.7		W 1659	0.5
	2313	1.5		2358	1.7
3	0457	0.6	**18**	0534	0.5
	1200	1.3		1244	1.5
	W 1704	0.8		TH 1803	0.6
4	0006	1.4	**19**	0058	1.6
	0557	0.6		0642	0.5
	TH 1306	1.3		F 1356	1.5
	1823	0.8		1915	0.7
5	0117	1.4	**20**	0214	1.5
	0706	0.6		0756	0.6
	F 1418	1.4		SA 1514	1.6
	1939	0.8		2033	0.7
6	0234	1.4	**21**	0336	1.6
	0808	0.6		0909	0.5
	SA 1525	1.5		SU 1623	1.7
	2040	0.7		2143	0.6
7	0343	1.5	**22**	0448	1.6
	0902	0.5		1009	0.5
	SU 1623	1.7		M 1723	1.8
	2132	0.6		2238	0.5
8	0444	1.6	**23**	0551	1.7
	0952	0.4		1059	0.4
	M 1716	1.8		TU 1816	1.9
	2220	0.5		2325	0.4
9	0540	1.7	**24**	0644	1.8
	1041	0.3		1144	0.4
	TU 1806	1.9		W 1903	2.0
	2306	0.4		○	
10	0633	1.8	**25**	0008	0.3
	1128	0.3		0730	1.8
	W 1854	2.0		TH 1225	0.3
	● 2352	0.3		1944	2.1
11	0723	1.9	**26**	0048	0.3
	1215	0.2		0809	1.9
	TH 1940	2.1		F 1303	0.3
				2020	2.1
12	0037	0.3	**27**	0127	0.2
	0809	1.9		0842	1.8
	F 1301	0.2		SA 1340	0.3
	2023	2.1		2049	2.0
13	0122	0.2	**28**	0204	0.2
	0853	1.9		0908	1.8
	SA 1346	0.2		SU 1414	0.3
	2114	2.1		2114	1.9
14	0207	0.2	**29**	0238	0.3
	0934	1.9		0932	1.7
	SU 1431	0.3		M 1444	0.4
	2144	2.0		2141	1.8
15	0254	0.2	**30**	0306	0.3
	1014	1.8		0959	1.6
	M 1517	0.3		TU 1507	0.5
	2224	1.9		2208	1.6
			31	0327	0.4
				1029	1.5
				W 1527	0.5
				2235	1.5

AUGUST

Day	Time	m	Day	Time	m
1	0351	0.5	**16**	0501	0.5
	1104	1.4		1205	1.6
	TH 1558	0.6		F 1728	0.6
	2306	1.4			
2	0429	0.5	**17**	0022	1.5
	1152	1.3		0606	0.6
	F 1650	0.7		SA 1316	1.5
	2355	1.3		1847	0.8
3	0529	0.6	**18**	0142	1.4
	1302	1.3		0734	0.7
	SA 1810	0.8		SU 1452	1.5
				2030	0.8
4	0120	1.3	**19**	0328	1.4
	0652	0.6		0902	0.7
	SU 1430	1.4		M 1612	1.6
	1946	0.8		2143	0.7
5	0301	1.4	**20**	0447	1.5
	0819	0.6		1001	0.6
	M 1547	1.6		TU 1713	1.8
	2104	0.7		2232	0.6
6	0418	1.5	**21**	0545	1.6
	0928	0.5		1046	0.5
	TU 1650	1.7		W 1803	1.9
	2202	0.5		2312	0.4
7	0522	1.7	**22**	0633	1.8
	1024	0.4		1126	0.4
	W 1747	1.9		TH 1847	2.0
	2253	0.4		○ 2350	0.3
8	0620	1.8	**23**	0714	1.9
	1115	0.3		1203	0.3
	TH 1840	2.1		F 1926	2.1
	● 2341	0.3			
9	0713	2.0	**24**	0027	0.2
	1203	0.2		0749	1.9
	F 1929	2.2		SA 1241	0.2
				1958	2.1
10	0027	0.1	**25**	0104	0.2
	0800	2.1		0818	1.9
	SA 1249	0.1		SU 1317	0.2
	2014	2.3		2026	2.1
11	0112	0.1	**26**	0139	0.1
	0842	2.1		0842	1.9
	SU 1333	0.1		M 1350	0.2
	2055	2.3		2051	2.0
12	0156	0.0	**27**	0210	0.1
	0921	2.1		0905	1.8
	M 1416	0.1		TU 1417	0.2
	2134	2.2		2116	1.9
13	0239	0.1	**28**	0232	0.3
	0958	2.0		0929	1.7
	TU 1458	0.2		W 1435	0.3
	2211	2.1		2140	1.7
14	0323	0.2	**29**	0246	0.3
	1035	1.9		0952	1.6
	W 1542	0.3		TH 1451	0.3
	2248	1.9		2201	1.5
15	0409	0.3	**30**	0305	0.4
	1116	1.7		1017	1.5
	TH 1629	0.5		F 1514	0.5
	2330	1.7		2224	1.4
			31	0335	0.5
				1052	1.4
				SA 1553	0.6
				2301	1.3

Extract D – Tides: Plymouth

TIME ZONE (UTC)
For Summer Time add ONE hour.

ENGLAND – PLYMOUTH
LAT 50°22′N   LONG 4°11′W
TIMES AND HEIGHTS OF HIGH AND LOW WATERS

MAY

Day	Time m	Time m	Time m	Time m
1 W	0223 0.8	0832 5.1	1442 1.1	2038 5.1
2 TH	0301 1.2	0906 4.8	1519 1.5	2107 4.8
3 F	0342 1.6	0941 4.4	1602 2.0	2144 4.5
4 SA	0433 2.0	1035 4.1	1657 2.3	2242 4.3
5 SU	0539 2.2	1226 4.0	1809 2.4	
6 M	0043 4.2	0706 2.2	1342 4.1	1939 2.3
7 TU	0159 4.3	0830 2.0	1439 4.3	2052 2.0
8 W	0254 4.6	0923 1.6	1526 4.6	2142 1.7
9 TH	0340 4.8	1006 1.4	1606 4.8	2224 1.4
10 F	0421 5.0	1045 1.1	1645 5.0	2302 1.2
11 SA	0501 5.1	1120 1.0	1722 5.1	2336 1.0
12 SU ●	0540 5.1	1153 1.0	1759 5.2	
13 M	0009 1.0	0617 5.1	1226 1.0	1834 5.2
14 TU	0041 1.0	0654 5.1	1258 1.0	1907 5.2
15 W	0113 1.0	0728 5.0	1329 1.1	1938 5.1
16 TH	0146 1.1	0802 4.9	1403 1.3	2012 5.1
17 F	0223 1.3	0840 4.8	1440 1.5	2052 4.9
18 SA	0306 1.5	0926 4.6	1528 1.7	2142 4.8
19 SU	0403 1.7	1024 4.4	1633 1.9	2243 4.6
20 M	0520 1.8	1137 4.4	1755 2.0	
21 TU	0000 4.6	0644 1.7	1303 4.4	1917 1.8
22 W	0125 4.7	0800 1.5	1417 4.7	2030 1.5
23 TH	0237 5.0	0906 1.2	1518 5.0	2132 1.2
24 F	0337 5.2	1003 0.8	1611 5.2	2226 0.9
25 SA	0430 5.4	1054 0.6	1659 5.4	2316 0.6
26 SU ○	0520 5.5	1141 0.5	1745 5.5	
27 M	0001 0.5	0607 5.4	1225 0.5	1828 5.5
28 TU	0045 0.6	0651 5.4	1306 0.7	1908 5.4
29 W	0126 0.7	0734 5.2	1345 0.9	1944 5.3
30 TH	0206 1.0	0812 5.0	1423 1.2	2016 5.1
31 F	0245 1.3	0847 4.7	1501 1.6	2047 4.9

JUNE

Day	Time m	Time m	Time m	Time m
1 SA	0325 1.6	0923 4.5	1542 1.9	2125 4.7
2 SU	0411 1.9	1009 4.2	1630 2.1	2215 4.5
3 M	0505 2.1	1116 4.1	1728 2.3	2321 4.3
4 TU	0608 2.1	1236 4.1	1834 2.3	
5 W	0046 4.3	0713 2.0	1341 4.3	1940 2.1
6 TH	0155 4.4	0815 1.8	1434 4.5	2040 1.9
7 F	0251 4.6	0908 1.6	1522 4.7	2132 1.6
8 SA	0340 4.8	0955 1.4	1607 4.9	2218 1.4
9 SU	0427 4.9	1038 1.2	1650 5.0	2300 1.2
10 M ●	0511 5.0	1119 1.0	1731 5.1	2340 1.1
11 TU	0553 5.0	1159 1.1	1811 5.2	
12 W	0020 1.0	0634 5.0	1239 1.1	1849 5.2
13 TH	0101 1.0	0715 5.0	1319 1.1	1927 5.2
14 F	0142 1.0	0756 5.0	1400 1.2	2007 5.2
15 SA	0225 1.1	0840 4.9	1444 1.3	2050 5.1
16 SU	0312 1.2	0927 4.8	1532 1.4	2138 5.0
17 M	0405 1.4	1020 4.7	1627 1.6	2234 4.9
18 TU	0505 1.5	1123 4.6	1732 1.7	2340 4.8
19 W	0614 1.5	1233 4.6	1843 1.7	
20 TH	0054 4.8	0725 1.5	1343 4.7	1955 1.6
21 F	0206 4.8	0834 1.4	1446 4.8	2102 1.4
22 SA	0310 4.9	0936 1.2	1544 5.0	2202 1.2
23 SU	0408 5.1	1031 1.0	1636 5.2	2255 1.0
24 M ○	0500 5.1	1120 0.9	1724 5.3	2343 0.9
25 TU	0549 5.2	1205 0.9	1808 5.3	
26 W	0029 0.8	0634 5.1	1250 0.9	1848 5.3
27 TH	0112 0.9	0716 5.0	1330 1.1	1925 5.2
28 F	0152 1.0	0755 4.9	1408 1.2	1959 5.1
29 SA	0230 1.2	0830 4.7	1444 1.4	2032 5.0
30 SU	0307 1.4	0904 4.6	1520 1.6	2108 4.8

JULY

Day	Time m	Time m	Time m	Time m
1 M	0343 1.6	0942 4.5	1557 1.8	2148 4.7
2 TU	0424 1.8	1027 4.3	1640 2.0	2235 4.5
3 W	0512 2.0	1121 4.2	1734 2.1	2332 4.4
4 TH	0609 2.0	1225 4.2	1837 2.2	
5 F	0040 4.3	0710 2.0	1332 4.3	1940 2.1
6 SA	0153 4.4	0811 1.8	1434 4.5	2040 1.9
7 SU	0258 4.5	0908 1.6	1530 4.7	2137 1.6
8 M	0354 4.7	1001 1.4	1620 4.9	2229 1.4
9 TU	0445 4.9	1051 1.3	1706 5.1	2318 1.2
10 W ●	0533 5.0	1139 1.1	1751 5.2	
11 TH	0005 1.0	0618 5.1	1227 1.0	1834 5.3
12 F	0052 0.8	0705 5.1	1313 0.9	1918 5.4
13 SA	0138 0.8	0751 5.1	1357 0.9	2002 5.4
14 SU	0223 0.8	0836 5.1	1441 0.9	2046 5.4
15 M	0308 0.9	0921 5.0	1525 1.1	2132 5.3
16 TU	0353 1.0	1008 4.9	1611 1.2	2220 5.1
17 W	0442 1.2	1100 4.7	1703 1.5	2315 4.9
18 TH	0539 1.5	1200 4.6	1805 1.7	
19 F	0021 4.7	0646 1.7	1309 4.6	1918 1.8
20 SA	0136 4.6	0801 1.7	1418 4.6	2035 1.7
21 SU	0248 4.6	0913 1.6	1522 4.8	2144 1.6
22 M	0351 4.7	1015 1.4	1618 5.0	2242 1.3
23 TU	0446 4.9	1107 1.2	1708 5.1	2332 1.1
24 W ○	0534 5.0	1154 1.1	1751 5.2	
25 TH	0017 1.0	0618 5.0	1237 1.0	1831 5.3
26 F	0100 0.9	0658 5.0	1316 1.0	1907 5.3
27 SA	0138 1.0	0734 4.9	1351 1.1	1940 5.2
28 SU	0211 1.1	0807 4.9	1423 1.2	2013 5.1
29 M	0242 1.2	0839 4.8	1451 1.4	2046 5.0
30 TU	0309 1.4	0912 4.7	1518 1.6	2119 4.8
31 W	0337 1.6	0947 4.5	1546 1.8	2154 4.6

AUGUST

Day	Time m	Time m	Time m	Time m
1 TH	0410 1.8	1027 4.4	1623 2.0	2235 4.5
2 F	0457 2.0	1117 4.3	1723 2.2	2330 4.3
3 SA	0607 2.1	1223 4.2	1845 2.2	
4 SU	0045 4.2	0722 2.1	1342 4.3	1959 2.1
5 M	0215 4.3	0831 1.9	1455 4.6	2105 1.8
6 TU	0327 4.6	0933 1.6	1554 4.8	2205 1.5
7 W	0424 4.8	1031 1.3	1645 5.1	2301 1.1
8 TH ●	0515 5.0	1124 1.0	1732 5.3	2352 0.8
9 F	0603 5.2	1214 0.8	1819 5.5	
10 SA	0041 0.6	0650 5.3	1302 0.6	1905 5.6
11 SU	0127 0.5	0737 5.3	1346 0.6	1950 5.6
12 M	0211 0.4	0821 5.3	1428 0.6	2034 5.6
13 TU	0252 0.6	0904 5.3	1508 0.8	2116 5.4
14 W	0332 0.9	0946 5.1	1548 1.0	2159 5.2
15 TH	0414 1.2	1031 4.9	1633 1.4	2246 4.8
16 F	0502 1.6	1125 4.6	1729 1.8	2349 4.5
17 SA	0605 1.9	1237 4.4	1844 2.1	
18 SU	0113 4.3	0732 2.1	1356 4.4	2019 2.1
19 M	0235 4.4	0902 2.0	1507 4.6	2136 1.8
20 TU	0342 4.5	1006 1.7	1605 4.8	2233 1.5
21 W	0435 4.7	1056 1.4	1653 5.1	2321 1.2
22 TH ○	0520 4.9	1140 1.1	1734 5.2	
23 F	0003 1.0	0559 5.0	1221 1.0	1810 5.3
24 SA	0042 0.9	0635 5.1	1257 0.9	1844 5.3
25 SU	0116 0.9	0708 5.1	1328 1.0	1917 5.3
26 M	0145 1.0	0739 5.0	1355 1.1	1948 5.2
27 TU	0210 1.1	0809 5.0	1418 1.3	2019 5.1
28 W	0231 1.3	0839 4.8	1437 1.4	2047 4.9
29 TH	0252 1.5	0908 4.7	1459 1.6	2114 4.7
30 F	0317 1.7	0939 4.5	1529 1.9	2147 4.5
31 SA	0352 1.9	1021 4.4	1614 2.1	2238 4.3

Extract E – Tidal Curves: Dover

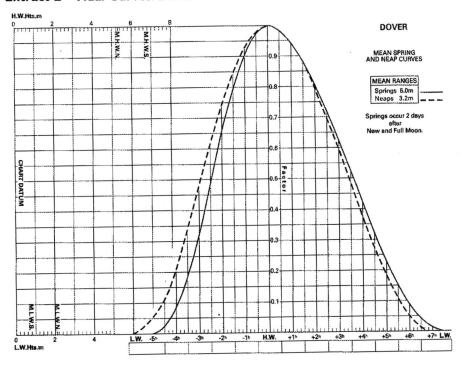

Extract F – Tidal Curves: Lymington/Yarmouth

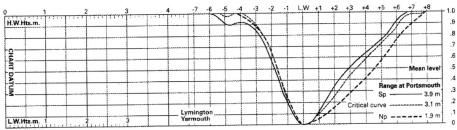

Extract G – Tidal Curves: Bucklers Hard

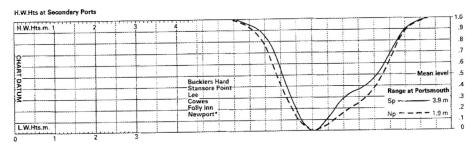

Extract H – Tidal Curves: Portland

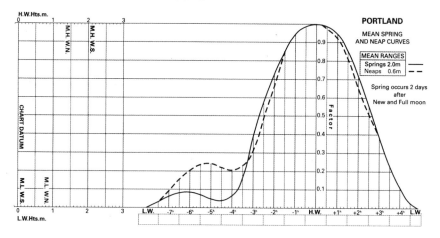

H.W.Hts.m.

PORTLAND

MEAN SPRING AND NEAP CURVES

MEAN RANGES
Springs 2.0m —
Neaps 0.6m ‑ ‑

Spring occurs 2 days after New and Full moon

M.H.W.N. M.H.W.S. CHART DATUM M.L.W.S. M.L.W.N. Factor

L.W.Hts.m.

Extract I – Port Information: Ramsgate

RAMSGATE 9.3.16

Kent 51°19´·51N 01°25´·50E ✳✳✳✿✿✦✦☆☆☆☆

CHARTS AC *5605*, 1827, *1828, 323*; Imray C1, C8, C30, 2100 series; Stan 5, 9, 20; OS 179

TIDES +0030 Dover; ML 2·7; Duration 0530; Zone 0 (UT)

Standard Port DOVER (←—)

Times				Height (metres)			
High Water		Low Water		MHWS	MHWN	MLWN	MLWS
0000	0600	0100	0700	6·8	5·3	2·1	0·8
1200	1800	1300	1900				
Differences RAMSGATE							
+0030	+0030	+0017	+0007	−1·6	−1·3	−0·7	−0·2
RICHBOROUGH							
+0015	+0015	+0030	+0030	−3·4	−2·6	−1·7	−0·7

HW Broadstairs = HW Dover +0037 approx.

SHELTER Options (a) inner marina, min depth 3m. Access approx HW ±2 via flap gate and lifting bridge, (b) W marina in 3m access H24, (c) E marina, in 2m, access H24. Larger vessels can berth on outer wavebreak pontoons of both W and E marinas.

NAVIGATION WPT 51°19´·43N 01°27´·70E, 090°/270° from/to S bkwtr,1·45M. Ferries use the well-marked main E-W chan dredged 7·5m, 110m wide; as lower chartlet). For ent/dep yachts must use the Recommended Yacht Track on the S side of the main buoyed chan.

Enter/dep under power, or advise Port Control if unable to motor. Ent/dep Royal Hbr directly; do not manoeuvre in the outer hbr. Holding area to the S of the S bkwtr must be used by yachts to keep the hbr ent clear for ferry tfc. Beware Dike Bank to the N and Quern Bank close S of the chan. Cross Ledge and Brake shoals are further S. Speed limit 5kn.

LIGHTS AND MARKS Ldg lts 270°: front Dir Oc WRG 10s 10m 5M, G259°-269°, W269°-271°, R271°-281°; rear, Oc 5s 17m 5M. N bkwtr hd = QG 10m 5M; S bkwtr hd = VQ R 10m 5M. At E Pier, **IPTS** (Sigs 2 and 3) visible from seaward and from within Royal Hbr, control appr into hbr limits (abeam Nos 1 & 2 buoys) and ent/exit to/from Royal Hbr. In addition a Fl Orange lt = ferry is under way; **no other vessel may enter Hbr limits from seaward or leave Royal Hbr.** Ent to inner marina controlled by separate IPTS to stbd of ent. Siren sounded approx 10 mins before gate closes; non-opening indicated by R ● or ●.

RADIO TELEPHONE Call Ramsgate Port Control Ch14 for clearance to enter or leave Royal Hbr. When in Royal Hbr call Ramsgate Marina Ch 80 for a berth. Ramsgate Dock Office can be called Ch14 for information on Inner Marina Lock.

TELEPHONE (Dial code 01843) Hr Mr 572100, 🖷 590941; Broadstairs Hr Mr 861879; ⊖ (01304) 224251 (H24); MRCC (01304) 210008; Marinecall 09068 500 455/456; Police 231055; Dr 852853; Ⓗ 225544.

FACILITIES Marinas (500+300 visitors) £1.60, 🕾592277, 🖷590941, www.ramsgatemarina.co.uk, AC, FW, C (10 ton), Ⓔ, ME, El, Sh, CH, ACA, Gaz, SM, 🚽; **Royal Hbr** P & D. **Royal Temple YC** 🕾 591766, Bar. **Town**; Gas, Gaz, V, R, Bar, ⊠, Ⓑ, ≈, ✈ (Manston).

Extract J – Port Information: Folkestone

FOLKESTONE 9.3.13

Kent 51°04´·59N 01°11´·67E ✳✳✿✦✦☆☆

CHARTS AC *5605, 1991, 1892*; Imray C8, C12; Stanfords 9, 20; OS 179

TIDES −0010 Dover; ML 3·9; Duration 0500; Zone 0 (UT)

Standard Port DOVER (—→)

Times				Height (metres)			
High Water		Low Water		MHWS	MHWN	MLWN	MLWS
0000	0600	0100	0700	6·8	5·3	2·1	0·8
1200	1800	1300	1900				
Differences FOLKESTONE							
−0020	−0005	−0010	−0010	+0·4	+0·4	0·0	−0·1
DUNGENESS							
−0010	−0015	−0020	−0010	+1·0	+0·6	+0·4	+0·1

SHELTER Good except in strong E-S winds when seas break at the hbr ent. Inner Hbr, dries 1·7m, has many FVs and local shoal draft boats, so limited room for visitors; access approx HW±2. Four Y waiting ⚓s lie ESE of ent to inner hbr in enough water for

1·5m draft to stay afloat. Berth on S Quay; fender board needed. Depth gauge on hd of E Pier. Ferry area is prohib to yachts; no room to ⚓ off. Beware High Speed Ferries.

NAVIGATION WPT 51°04´·33N 01°11´·88E, 150°/330° from/to bkwtr hd lt, 0·26M. Beware drying Mole Hd Rks and Copt Rks to stbd of the ent; from/to the NE, keep well clear of the latter due to extended sewer outfall pipe.

LIGHTS AND MARKS Hotel block is conspic at W end of Inner Hbr. Ldg lts 295° at ferry terminal, FR and FG (occas). QG lt at E pierhead on brg 305° leads to inner hbr. Bu flag or 3 ● (vert) at FS on S arm, 5 mins before ferry sails = hbr closed. 3● (vert) = enter.

RADIO TELEPHONE Call *Folkestone Port Control* VHF Ch 15, 16.

TELEPHONE (Dial code 01303) Hr Mr 220544 (H24), 🖷 221567; MRCC (01304) 210008; ⊖ (01304) 224251; Marinecall 09068 500456; Police 850055.

FACILITIES S Quay BR Slipway £10 for AB or ⚓, Slip (free), FW; **Folkestone Y & MB Club** 🕾 251574, D, FW, L, Slip, M, Bar, 🚽. **Town** EC Wed (larger shops open all day); P & D (cans, 100 yds), V, R, Bar, ⊠, Ⓑ, ≈, ✈ (Lydd). Freight ferries and Hoverspeed (Seacat) to Boulogne.

Extract K – Port Information: Yarmouth

YARMOUTH *9.2.19*

Isle of Wight **50°42'·42N 01°30'·05W** ✵✵✵⊛⌇⌇🏠🏠🏠

CHARTS AC *5600, 2021, 2037*; Imray C3, C15; Stanfords 11, 24, 25; OS 196

TIDES Sp −0050, +0150, Np +0020 Dover; ML 2·0; Zone 0 (UT)

Standard Port PORTSMOUTH (⟶)

Times				Height (metres)			
High Water		Low Water		MHWS	MHWN	MLWN	MLWS
0000	0600	0500	1100	4·7	3·8	1·9	0·8
1200	1800	1700	2300				
Differences YARMOUTH							
−0105	+0005	−0025	−0030	−1·7	−1·2	−0·3	0·0

NOTE: Double HWs occur at or near sp; at other times there is a stand lasting about two hrs. Predictions refer to the first HW when there are two; otherwise to the middle of the stand. See 9.2.12.

SHELTER Good from all directions of wind and sea, but swell enters if wind strong from N/NE. Hbr dredged 2m from ent to bridge; access H24. Moor fore-and-aft on piles, on the Town Quay, or on pontoon. Boats over 15m LOA, 4m beam or 2·4m draft should give notice of arrival. Berthing on S Quay is normally only for fuel, C, FW, or to load people/cargo. Hbr gets very full in season and may be closed to visitors signalled by R flag and notice. 36 Y 🛥s outside hbr (see chartlet) and ⚓ further to the N or S.

NAVIGATION WPT 50°42'·58N 01°30'·01W, 008°/188° from/to abeam car ferry terminal, 2ca. Dangers on appr are Black Rock (SHM buoy Fl G 5s) and shoal water to the N of the E/W bkwtr. Beware ferries. Caution: strong ebb in the ent at sp. Speed limit 4kn in hbr and 6kn in approaches. ⚓ prohib in hbr and beyond R Yar road bridge. This swing bridge opens for 10 mins for access to the moorings and BYs up-river at Saltern Quay: (May-Sept) 0800, 0900, 1000, 1200, 1400, 1600, 1730, 1830, 2000LT; and on request (Oct-May). The river is navigable by dinghy at HW almost up to Freshwater.
A **Historic Wreck** (see 9.0.3h) is at 50°42'·55N 01°29'·67W, 2ca ExN from ent of pier; marked by Y SPM buoy.

LIGHTS AND MARKS Ldg bns (2 W ◇ on B/W masts) and ldg lts (FG 5/9m 2M), on quay, 188°. When hbr is closed to visitors (eg when full in summer or at week-ends) a R flag is flown at the pier head and an illuminated board 'Harbour Full' is displayed at the ent, plus an extra ●. In fog a high intensity ⓦ lt is shown from the pier hd and from the inner E pier, together with a .

RADIO TELEPHONE Hr Mr VHF Ch 68. Water Taxi Ch 15.

TELEPHONE (Dial code 01983 = code for whole of IOW) Hr Mr 760321, 🖷 761192; MRSC (023 92) 552100; ⊖ 0345 231110 (H24); Marinecall 0898 500457; Police 52800; Dr 760434.

FACILITIES Hbr £9.00 (30ft) (£4 < 4hrs) on piles, Town Quay, pontoon or 🛥; Slip, P, D, L, M, Gaz, FW, C (5 ton), Ice, 🅾, 🅰;
Yarmouth SC ☎ 760512, Bar, L;
Royal Solent YC ☎ 760256, Bar, R, L, Slip;
Services Note: BY in SW corner but most marine services/BYs are located near Salterns Quay, 500m up-river above the bridge, or ½M by road. BY, Slip, M, ME, El, Sh, CH, Gas, Gaz, LPG, SM, C, Divers.
Town EC Wed; V, R, Bar, ✉, Ⓑ (May-Sept 1000-1445, Sept-May a.m. only), ≠ (Lymington), ✈ (Bournemouth/Southampton).

Extract L – Port Information: Lymington

LYMINGTON *9.2.20*

Hampshire **50°45'·13N 01·31'·40W** ✵✵⊛⌇⌇⌇🏠🏠

CHARTS AC *5600, 2021, 2035*; Imray C3, C15; Stanfords 11, 25, 25; OS 196

TIDES Sp −0040, +0100, Np +0020 Dover; ML 2·0; Zone 0 (UT)

Standard Port PORTSMOUTH (⟶)

Times				Height (metres)			
High Water		Low Water		MHWS	MHWN	MLWN	MLWS
0000	0600	0500	1100	4·7	3·8	1·9	0·8
1200	1800	1700	2300				
Differences LYMINGTON							
−0110	+0005	−0020	−0020	−1·7	−1·2	−0·5	−0·1

NOTE: Double HWs occur at or near sp and on other occasions there is a stand lasting about 2hrs. Predictions refer to the first HW when there are two. At other times they refer to the middle of the stand. See 9.2.12.

SHELTER Good in two large marinas and at Customs House Quay and Town Quay; the latter provide public AB (see Hr Mr) and up to 100 🛥s (W). River is accessible at all states of the tide; speed limit 4kn. ⚓ in the river is prohib, but in off-shore winds yachts can ⚓ off the mud flats outside.

NAVIGATION WPT 50°44'·23N 01°30'·36W, 139·5°/319·5° from/to abeam Nos 1 and 2 piles, 1·9ca. There are extensive, but well marked mud banks around the ent. Entering, leave Jack- in-the-Basket about 45m to port to clear Cross Boom.
Min depth 1·8m in mid-chan from ent to Railway Pier; thence 1·1m to Town Quay. All craft must give way to and keep clear of ferries in very narrow chan; beware wave screens off Lymington Yacht Haven.

LIGHTS AND MARKS Ldg lts 319°, both FR 12/17m 8M. Ent marked by Jack-in-the-Basket, Fl R 2s, and by conspic YC starting platform, 60m E of No 1 bn, Fl G 2s. Narrow chan is marked by 8 PHM piles (four Fl R 2s) and 9 SHM piles (eight Fl G 2s). Two sets of ldg marks/lts on the central section ensure lateral clearance between opposite direction ferries: two BW posts, Dir FW, on flats to SE of Cage Boom in line at 007°30' for inbound ferries; two RW posts, Dir FW, on flats to SSE of Seymours Post in line at 187°30' for outbound ferries.
Harper's Post ECM by, Q (3) 10s 5m 1M, and two FY ldg lts 244° mark the ent into Lymington Yacht Haven.

RADIO TELEPHONE Marinas VHF Ch **80** M (office hrs).

TELEPHONE (Dial code 01590) Hr Mr 672014; MRSC (023 92) 552100; ⊖ 0345 231110 (H24); Marinecall 09068 500457; Police 675411; Dr 672953; Ⓗ 677011.

FACILITIES Marinas:
Lymington Yacht Haven (475+100 visitors), 2m depth, all tides access, ☎ 677071, 🖷 678186, £1.87, P, D, AC, FW, BY, ME, El, Sh, C (10 ton), BH (40 ton), CH, Gas, Gaz, LPG, 🅾, 🅰 🚻 (mobile) ;
Lymington Marina (300+100 visitors), ☎ 673312, 🖷 676353, £2.22, Slip, P, AC, D, FW, ME, El, Sh, CH, BH (100 ton), C, (37, 80 ton), Gas, Gaz, 🅾, 🅰;
Town Quay AB £1.05, M, FW, Slip (see Hr Mr); **Bath Road** public pontoon, FW, 🅰.
Clubs: Royal Lymington YC ☎ 672677, R, Bar, 🅰; **Lymington Town SC** ☎ 674514, AB, R, Bar.
Services: M, FW, ME, El, Sh, C (16 ton), CH, Ⓔ, SM, ACA.
Town every facility including ✉, Ⓑ, ≠, ✈ (Bournemouth or Southampton).

Extract M – Port Information: Beaulieu

BEAULIEU RIVER 9.2.22

Hampshire 50°46'·89N 01°21'·72W (Ent) ✹✹⚓⚓⚓🏠🏠🏠

CHARTS AC *5600, 2021, 2035, 2036*; Imray C3, C15; Stanfords 11, 24, 25; OS 196

TIDES –0100 and +0140 Dover; ML 2·4; Zone 0 (UT)

Standard Port PORTSMOUTH (→)

Times				Height (metres)			
High Water		Low Water		MHWS	MHWN	MLWN	MLWS
0000	0600	0500	1100	4·7	3·8	1·9	0·8
1200	1800	1700	2300				
BUCKLER'S HARD							
–0040	–0010	+0010	–0010	–1·0	–0·8	–0·2	–0·3
STANSORE POINT							
–0050	–0010	–0005	–0010	–0·8	–0·5	–0·3	–0·1

NOTE: Double HWs occur at or near springs; the 2nd HW is approx 1¾ hrs after the 1st. On other occasions there is a stand which lasts about two hrs. The predictions refer to the first HW when there are two, or to the middle of the stand. See 9.2.12.

SHELTER Very good in all winds. ⚓ possible in reach between Lepe Ho and Beaulieu River SC, but preferable to proceed to Buckler's Hard Yacht Hbr (AB and ◐ pile moorings).
Many of the landing stages/slips shown on the chartlet (and AC 2021) are privately owned and not to be used. The uppermost reaches of the river are best explored first by dinghy due to the lack of channel markers and the short duration of the HW stand.
Rabies: Craft with animals from abroad are prohibited in the river.

NAVIGATION WPT 50°46'·53N 01°21'·33W, 144°/324° from/to abeam Beaulieu Spit dolphin (Fl R 5s), 4ca. Ent dangerous LW±2.
There are patches drying 0·3m approx 100m S of Beaulieu Spit. 1ca further SSE, close W of the ldg line, are shoal depths 0·1m. Lepe Spit SCM buoy, Q (6) + L Fl 15s, is 7ca E of Beaulieu Spit dolphin at 50°46'.78N 01°20'·63W.
The swatchway off Beaulieu River SC is closed. A speed limit of 5kn applies to the whole river.

LIGHTS AND MARKS Ldg marks at ent 324° must be aligned exactly due to shoal water either side of ldg line. The front is No 2 bn, R with Or dayglow topmark, △ shape above □; the rear is Lepe Ho. Beaulieu Spit, R dolphin with W band, Fl R 5s 3M vis 277°-037°; ra refl, should be left approx 40m to port. The old CG cottages and Boat House are conspic, approx 320m E of Lepe Ho.
The river is clearly marked by R and G bns and perches. SHM bns 5, 9, 19 and 21 are all Fl G 4s; PHM bns 12 & 20 are Fl R 4s. Marina pontoons A, C and E have 2FR (vert).

RADIO TELEPHONE None.

TELEPHONE (Dial code 01590) Hr Mr 616200/616234, 🖷 616211; MRSC (023 92) 552100; ⊖ 0345 231110 (H24); Marinecall 09068 500457; Police (023 80) 335444; Dr 612451 or (023 80) 845955; Ⓗ 77011.

FACILITIES Buckler's Hard Yacht Hbr £2.20 (110+20 ◐) ☎ 616200, 🖷 616211, Slip, M (£1 on piles), P, D, AC, FW, ME, El, Sh, C (1 ton), BH (26 ton), SM, Gas, Gaz, CH, ◨, &, V, R, Bar.
Village V (Stores ☎ 616293), R, Bar, ✉ (Beaulieu), Ⓑ (Mon, Wed, Fri AM or Hythe), ⇌ (bus to Brockenhurst), → (Bournemouth or Southampton).

Extract N – Port Information: Newtown

NEWTOWN RIVER 9.2.21

Isle of Wight 50°43'·45N 01°24'·66W ✹✹⚓⚓🏠🏠

CHARTS AC *5600, 2021, 2035, 2036*; Imray C3, C15; Stanfords 11, 24, 25; OS 196

TIDES Sp –0108, Np +0058, Dover; ML 2·3; Zone 0 (UT)

Standard Port PORTSMOUTH (→)

Times				Height (metres)			
High Water		Low Water		MHWS	MHWN	MLWN	MLWS
0000	0600	0500	1100	4·7	3·8	1·9	0·8
1200	1800	1700	2300				
Differences SOLENT BANK (Data approximate)							
–0100	0000	–0015	–0020	–1·3	–1·0	–0·3	–0·1

NOTE: Double HWs occur at or near springs; at other times there is a stand which lasts about 2hrs. Predictions refer to the first HW when there are two. At other times they refer to the middle of the stand. See 9.2.12.

SHELTER 3½M E of Yarmouth, Newtown gives good shelter, but is exposed to N'ly winds. There are 6 ◓s (W) in Clamerkin Lake and 18 (W) in the main arm leading to Shalfleet Quay, R buoys are private all are numbered; check with Hr Mr.
Do not ⚓ beyond boards showing "Anchorage Limit" on account of oyster beds. Fin keel boats can stay afloat from ent to Hamstead landing or to Clamerkin Limit Boards.
Public landing on E side of river N of Newtown quay by conspic black boathouse. The whole eastern peninsula ending in Fishhouse Pt is a nature reserve; yachtsmen are asked not to land there. 5kn speed limit in hbr is strictly enforced.
If no room in river, good ⚓ in 3-5m W of ent, but beware rky ledges SSE of Hamstead Ledge SHM buoy, Fl (2) G 5s, and possible under water obstructions.
At Solent Bank (approx 50°44'·5N 01°25'·5W), 1M NW of Newtown ent, expect to see dredgers working.

NAVIGATION WPT 50°43'·83N 01°25'·18W, 310°/130° from/to ldg bn, 0·46M. From W, make good Hamstead Ledge SHM buoy, thence E to pick up ldg marks. From E, keep N of Newtown gravel banks where W/SW winds over a sp ebb can raise steep breaking seas; leave PHM Fl.R4s bar buoy to port. Best ent is from about HW –4, on the flood but while the mud flats are still visible. Ent lies between two shingle spits and can be rough in N winds especially near HW. There is only about 0·9m over the bar.
Inside the ent so many perches mark the mud banks that confusion may result. Near junction to Causeway Lake depth is only 0·9m and beyond this water quickly shoals.
At ent to Clamerkin Lake (1·2 -1·8m) keep to SE to avoid gravel spit off W shore, marked by two PHM perches; the rest of chan is marked by occas perches. Beware many oyster beds in Western Haven and Clamerkin Lake.
There is a rifle range at top of Clamerkin Lake and in Spur Lake; R flags flown during firing. High voltage power line across Clamerkin at 50°42'·81N 01°22'·66W has clearance of only 9m and no shore markings.

LIGHTS AND MARKS Conspic TV mast (152m) bearing about 150° (3.3M from hbr ent) provides initial approach track. In season a forest of masts inside the hbr are likely to be evident. The ldg bns, 130°, are off Fishhouse Pt in mud on NE side of ent: front bn, RW bands with Y-shaped topmark; rear bn, W with W disc inside. Once inside, there are no lights.

RADIO TELEPHONE None.

TELEPHONE (Dial code 01983 = code for whole of IOW) Hr Mr 531622; 🖷 531914; MRSC (023 92) 552100; ⊖ 0345 231110 (H24); Marinecall 09068 500457; Police 528000; Dr 760434; Taxi 884353.

FACILITIES Newtown Quay M £1.00 approx, L, FW; **Shalfleet Quay** Slip, M, L, AB; **Lower Hamstead Landing** L, FW; **R. Seabroke** ☎ 531213, Sh; **Shalfleet Village** V, Bar. **Newtown** ✉, Ⓑ (Yarmouth or Newport), ⇌ (bus to Yarmouth, ferry to Lymington), → (Bournemouth or Southampton).

Extract O – Port Information: Christchurch

CHRISTCHURCH 9.2.14

Dorset 50°43'·53N 01°44'·33W ❀❀❀❀⚓⚓✿✿✿

CHARTS AC *5601, 2172, 2035*; Imray C4; Stanfords 7, 12, 24; OS 195

TIDES HW Sp –0210, Np, –0140 Dover; ML 1·2; Zone 0 (UT)
Standard Port PORTSMOUTH (→)

Times				Height (metres)			
High Water		Low Water		MHWS	MHWN	MLWN	MLWS
0000	0600	0500	1100	4·7	3·8	1·9	0·8
1200	1800	1700	2300				
Differences BOURNEMOUTH							
–0240	+0055	–0050	–0030	–2·7	–2·2	–0·8	–0·3
CHRISTCHURCH (Entrance)							
–0230	+0030	–0035	–0035	–2·9	–2·4	–1·2	–0·2
CHRISTCHURCH (Quay)							
–0210	+0100	+0105	+0055	–2·9	–2·4	–1·0	0·0
CHRISTCHURCH (Tuckton bridge)							
–0205	+0110	+0110	+0105	–3·0	–2·5	–1·0	+0·1

NOTE: Double HWs occur, except near nps; predictions are for the higher HW. Near nps there is a stand; predictions are for mid-stand. Tidal levels are for inside the bar. Outside the bar the tide is about 0·6m lower at sp. Floods (or drought) in the Rivers Avon and Stour cause considerable variations from predicted hts. See 9.2.12.

SHELTER Good in lee of Hengistbury Hd, elsewhere exposed to SW winds. R Stour, navigable at HW up to Tuckton, and the R Avon up to the first bridge, give good shelter in all winds. Most ⌕s in the hbr dry. No ⌕ in chan. No berthing at ferry jetty by Mudeford sandbank. Hbr speed limit 4kn. Fishing licence obligatory.

NAVIGATION WPT 50°43'·53N 01°43'·58W, 090°/270° from/to NE end of Mudeford Quay 0·5M. The bar/chan is liable to shift. The ent is difficult on the ebb which reaches 4-5kn in 'The Run'. Recommended ent/dep at HW/stand. Chan inside hbr is narrow and mostly shallow (approx 0·3m) soft mud; mean ranges are 1·2m sp and 0·7m nps. Beware groynes S of Hengistbury Hd, Beerpan and Yarranton Rks.

LIGHTS AND MARKS 2 FG (vert) at NE end of Mudeford Quay. Unlit chan buoys in hbr and apps are locally laid April-Oct inc; info from ☎ 483250.

RADIO TELEPHONE None.

TELEPHONE (Dial code 01202) MRSC (01305) 760439; ⊖ 0345 231110 (H24); Marinecall 09068 500457; Police 486333; ⊞ 303626; Casualty 704167.

FACILITIES Elkins BY ☎ 483141, AB £15; **Rossiter Yachts** ☎ 483250, AB £14; **Christchurch SC (CSC)** ☎ 483150, limited AB £9.50, monohulls only, max LOA 9m.
Services: M*, L*, D, P (cans), FW, El, Sh, CH, ACA, Gas, C (10 ton), Slip. **Town** ⊠, ⑧, ≅, ✈ (Bournemouth).

Extract P – Port Information: Swanage/Studland

SWANAGE 9.2.11

Dorset 50°36'·81N 01°57'·05W ❀❀❀❀⚓⚓✿✿

CHARTS AC *5601, 2172, 2610, 2175*; Imray C4; Stanfords 7, 12, 15; OS 195

TIDES HW Sp –0235 & +0125, Np –0515 & +0120 on Dover; ML 1·5
Standard Port POOLE HARBOUR (→)

Times				Height (metres)			
High Water		Low Water		MHWS	MHWN	MLWN	MLWS
—	—	0500	1100	2·2	1·7	1·2	0·6
—	—	1700	2300				
Differences SWANAGE							
—	—	–0045	–0055	–0·2	–0·1	0·0	–0·1

NOTE: From Swanage to Christchurch double HWs occur except at nps. HW differences refer to the higher HW when there are two and are approximate.

SHELTER Good ⌕ in winds from SW to N, but bad in E/SE winds >F4 due to swell which may persist for 6 hrs after a blow. >F6 holding gets very difficult; Poole is nearest refuge. AB is feasible on S side of pier (open Apr-Oct) subject to wind and sea state; pleasure 'steamers' use the N side.

NAVIGATION WPT 50°36'·73N 01°56'·58W, 054°/234° from/to pier hd, 0·30M. Coming from S beware Peveril Ledge and its Race which can be vicious with a SW wind against the main ebb. It is best to keep 1M seaward of Durlston Head and Peveril Point. On the W side of Swanage Bay, keep clear of Tanville and Phippards Ledges, approx 300m offshore. To the S of the pier are the ruins of an old pier.

LIGHTS AND MARKS The only lts are 2 FR (vert) on the pier; difficult to see due to confusing street lts. Peveril Ledge PHM buoy is unlit and hard to pick out at night due to Anvil Pt lt; keep 0·5M clear of it to the E.

RADIO TELEPHONE None.

TELEPHONE (Dial code 01929) Pier 427058, mobile 0780 1616216; MRSC (01305) 760439; ⊖ 0345 231110 (H24) or (01202) 685157; Marinecall 09068 500457; Police 422004; Dr 422231; ⊞ 422202.

FACILITIES Pier, L*, FW, AB* £1, £3 for <3hrs; after 2100 gain access to pier from ashore via **Swanage SC** ☎ 422987, Slip, L, FW, Bar, ⌕; **Boat Park** (Peveril Pt), Slip, FW, L; **Services:** Diving. **Town** P & D (cans, 1¾M), FW, V, R, Bar, ⊠, ⑧, ≅ (bus connection to Wareham), ✈ (Hurn).

ADJACENT ANCHORAGE
STUDLAND BAY, Dorset, **50°38'·73N 01°55'·90W.** AC*2172, 2175*. Tides approx as for Swanage (9.2.11). Shelter is good except in N/E winds. Beware Redend Rocks off S shore. Best ⌕ in about 3m, 3ca NW of The Yards (three strange projections on the chalk cliffs near Handfast Pt).**Village:** EC Thurs; FW, V, R, ⊠, hotel, P&D (cans), No marine facilities. A Historic Wreck (see 9.0.3h) is at 50°39'·70N 01°54'·87W, 4·5ca NNE of Poole Bar Buoy.

EXTRACTS

Extract Q – Port Information: Weymouth

WEYMOUTH 9.2.9

Dorset 50°36′·57N 02°26′·58W ✲✲✲✷↻↻↻♻♻♻

CHARTS AC *5601*, 2172, 2268, 2255, *2610*; Imray C4, C5; Stanfords 7, 12; OS 194

TIDES –0438 Dover; ML 1·1; Zone 0 (UT)

Standard Port PORTLAND (←)

Predictions for Weymouth are as for Portland. Mean ranges are small: 0·6m at np and 2·0m at sp.
NOTE: Double LWs occur; predictions are for first LW. A LW stand lasts about 4 hrs at sp and 1 hr at nps.
Due to an eddy, the tidal stream in Weymouth Roads is W-going at all times except HW –0510 to HW –038.

SHELTER Good, but swell enters outer hbr and The Cove in strong E winds. Berthing options from seaward:
In The Cove on pontoon S side or N side (Custom House Quay) off RDYC; fender boards are available elsewhere. In season rafting-up is the rule. (The quays between The Cove and the lifting bridge are reserved for FVs).
The municipal pontoons just beyond the lifting bridge (see NAVIGATION) are for residents only; no visitors.
N of these Weymouth Marina, dredged 2·5m, has 300 berths in complete shelter.
It is feasible to ⚓ in Weymouth Bay, NE of hbr ent in about 3m, but necessarily some way offshore due to the drying sands and buoyed watersport areas inshore. See also 9.2.7 for possible ⚓ in Portland Harbour.

NAVIGATION WPT 50°36′·71N, 02°26′·18W 060°/240° from/to front ldg lt, 0·50M. The hbr ent lies deep in the NW corner of Weymouth Bay; it could in some conditions be confused with the N ent to Portland Hbr. Hbr speed limit is 'Dead Slow'. Comply with IPTS. High Speed Ferries operate in the area.
The **bridge** lifts (LT) 0800, 1000, 1200, 1400, 1600, 1800, 2000 and 2100 on request throughout the summer. 1 hr's notice by telephone is required for all lifts in the winter. Five mins before lift times, craft should be visible to the br, and listening on VHF Ch 12. 3FR or 3FG (vert) on both sides of the bridge are tfc lts, not navigational lts; outbound vessels usually take priority.

Waiting pontoons are close E of bridge on S side and also on the marina side. Clearances when the bridge is down are approx 2·7m MHWS, 3·8m MHWN, 4·6m MLWN, 5·2m MLWS. NOTE: If heading E, check Lulworth firing programme; see overleaf and the Supplements for current dates.

LIGHTS AND MARKS Conspic ✠ spire, 6ca NNW of hbr ent, is a useful daymark to help find the ent when approaching from SE past the Portland bkwtrs or from the E. Note: On the E side of Portland Hbr (see 9.2.7), approx 7ca ESE of 'D' Head lt, are 4 SPM lt buoys (marking a Noise range).
Portland 'A' Head lt Iho, Fl 10s 22m 20M, is 1·7M SE of hbr ent and provides the best initial guidance at night; it is also a conspic W tr. Caution: About 500m SE of Weymouth S Pier there are 3 SPM buoys (one Fl Y 2s) marking DG Range. Pierhead lts may be hard to see against shore lts.
Ldg lts 240°, 2 FR (H24), are 500m inside the pierhds; daymarks (same position) are R open ◇s on W poles; they are not visible until the hbr ent is opened.
IPTS must be obeyed. They are shown from a RW mast near the root of the S pier. There is one additional signal:
2 ● over 1 ● = Ent and dep prohib (ent obstructed).
If no sigs are shown, vessels are clear to enter or leave with caution.

RADIO TELEPHONE *Weymouth Harbour* VHF Ch 12 16 (0800-2000 in summer and when vessel due); *Weymouth Town Bridge* also on 12 (at opening times). *Weymouth Marina* Ch 80. Ch 60 for diesel.

TELEPHONE (Dial code 01305) Hr Mr 206423, 🖷 206422; Bridge 206423/789357; Marina 767576; MRSC 760439; Marinecall 09068 500457; ⊖ 01202 634500; Police 250512; Dr 774466; Ⓗ Weymouth (minor injuries only) 760022, Dorchester 251150.

FACILITIES (From seaward) Outer Hbr, The Cove, Custom House Quay (only at the latter: AC, showers free) AB £1.60 (£5.50 for <4 hrs), FW, M, Slip near WSC; Weymouth SC ☎ 785481, M, Bar; **Royal Dorset YC** ☎ 786258, M, Bar; **Marina** ☎ 767576, 🖷 767575; (237 inc Ⓥ) £2.20 (£5 for <5 hrs, 1000-1600), FW, AC; **Services:** CH, Sh, ACA, Gaz, Rigging, Slip, ME, Ⓔ, El, CH. D Raybar at Nelsons Wharf ☎ mobile 07860 912401, VHF Ch 60 or Quayside Fuel ☎ 01305 783567, mobile 07977 337620, VHF Ch 60. **Town** www.weymouth.gov.uk, P & D (cans), FW, 🖳, V, R, Bar, ⊠, Ⓑ, ≠, ✈ (Bournemouth).

Extract R – Port Information: Portland

PORTLAND HARBOUR 9.2.7

Dorset 50°35′·14N 02°24′·98W (E Ship Chan) ✲✲✲✷↻♻

CHARTS AC *5601*, 2268, 2255, *2610*; Imray C4, C5; Stanfords 7,12; OS 194

TIDES –0430 Dover; ML 1·0; Zone 0 (UTC)

Standard Port PORTLAND (→)

Times				Height (metres)			
High Water		Low Water		MHWS	MHWN	MLWN	MLWS
0100	0700	0100	0700	2·1	1·4	0·8	0·1
1300	1900	1300	1900				
LULWORTH COVE and MUPE BAY (Worbarrow Bay)							
+0005	+0015	–0005	0000	+0·1	+0·1	+0·2	+0·1

NOTE: Double LWs occur. Predictions are for the first LW. The Second LW occurs from 3 to 4 hrs later and may, at Springs, occasionally be lower than the first.

SHELTER Poor, due to lack of wind breaks ⚓ on W side of hbr in about 3m between ☆ Fl (4) 10s and ☆ L Fl 10s. E Fleet is only suitable for small craft with lowering masts. Better options for yachts are Weymouth hbr or marina.

NAVIGATION WPT 50°35′·10N 02°24′·08W, 090°/270° from/to E Ship Chan, Fort Hd, 0·50M. The S Chan is permanently closed. Speed limit in the hbr is 6kn in the areas

defined or within 150m of any breakwater or hbr premises. Vessels under 10m may exceed 12kn in the undefined areas. Beware rky reef extending 1ca off NE of Castle Cove SC, shoals E of Small Mouth and fast catamarans ex-Weymouth. 4 noise range lt buoys Fl.Y are 7ca SE of D Head and 3 degaussing buoys (1 lit) are 400m SE of Weymouth S Pier head. Portland Race (see 9.2.5 and 9.2.8) is extremely dangerous. Avoid the Shambles bank.

LIGHTS AND MARKS Bill of Portland (S end) Fl (4) 20s 43m 25M; W tr, R band. The number of flashes gradually changes from 4 to 1 in arc 221°-244°, and from 1 to 4 in arc 117°-141°. FR 19m 13M, same tr, vis 271°-291° (20°) over The Shambles, Dia 30s. Other lts on charlet.

RADIO TELEPHONE Monitor VHF Ch 74 for commercial ship movements. Port Ops Ch 14, 20, 28, 71, **74**.

TELEPHONE (Dial code 01305) Port Control 824044, 🖷 824055; Ⓗ824055; MRSC 760439; Marinecall 09066 526241; Police 768970; Dr (GP) 820422; Ⓗ (Emergency) 820341.

FACILITIES Hbr dues apply to yachts: £3.60 daily for 6 – 9.15m LOA. **Castle Cove SC** ☎ 783708, M, L, FW; **Services:** Slip, M, L, FW, ME, ✕, C, CH, El (mobile workshop). **The RYA Sailing Centre** (ex-Sailing Centre) hosts National and International events. **Town** www.portland-port.co.uk, ⊠, Ⓑ, ≠ (bus to Weymouth), ✈ (Bournemouth).

EXTRACTS

Extract S – Tidal Streams: Mid Channel

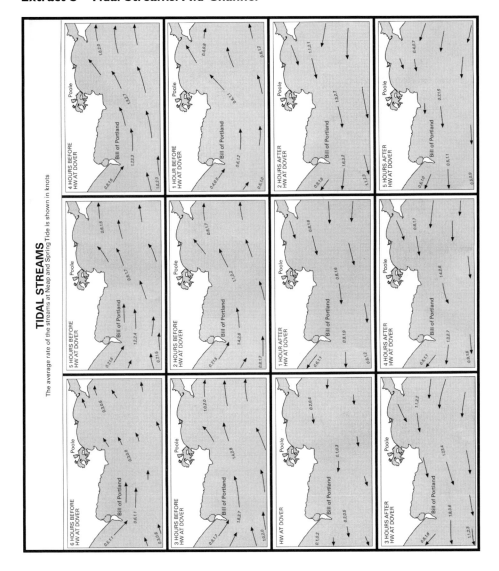

71

Extract T – Tidal Streams: Portland Bill

PORTLAND TIDAL STREAMS

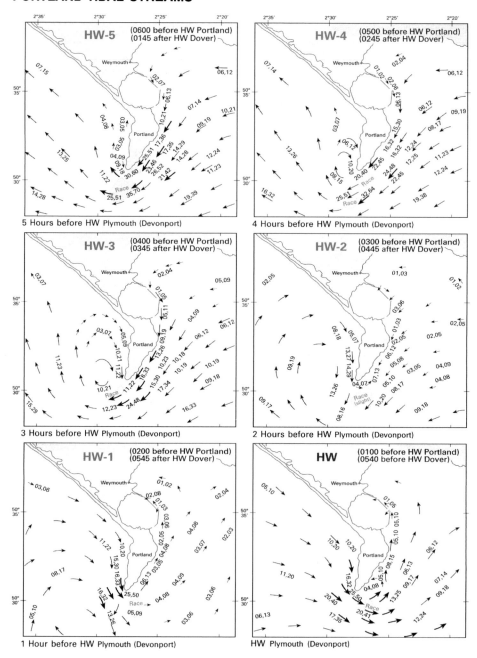

Extract T (continued) – Tidal Streams: Portland Bill

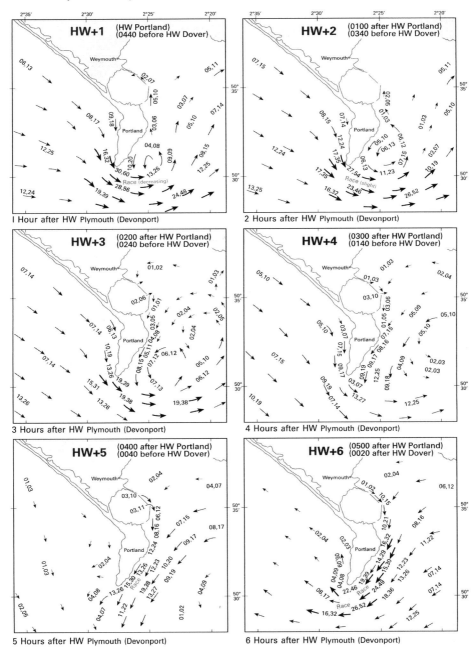

EXTRACTS

Extract U – Passage Information: Portland to Needles

9.2.5 PASSAGE INFORMATION

Reference books include: Admiralty *Channel Pilot*; *South Coast Cruising* (YM/Fishwick); *Shell Channel Pilot* (Imray/Cunliffe); and *Creeks and Harbours of the Solent* (Adlard Coles). See 9.0.6 for distances across the Channel, and 9.3.5 and 9.15.5 for notes on cross-Channel passages. Admiralty Small Craft Folio 5601 covers Portland to the Needles, contains 10 A2 size charts in a clear plastic wallet and costs £35.00 (2000). Encapsulated Solent and Chichester Hbr Racing Charts (Macmillan Reeds).

THE PORTLAND RACE (chart *2255*) South of the Bill lies Portland Race in which severe and very dangerous sea states occur. Even in settled weather it should be carefully avoided by small craft, although at neaps it may be barely perceptible.

The Race occurs at the confluence of two strong S-going tidal streams which run down each side of Portland for almost 10 hours out of 12 at springs. These streams meet the main E-W stream of the Channel, producing large eddies on either side of Portland and a highly confused sea state with heavy overfalls in the Race. The irregular contours of the sea-bed, which shoals abruptly from depths of over 100m some 2M south of the Bill to as little as 9m on Portland Ledge 1M further N, greatly contribute to the violence of the Race. Portland Ledge strongly deflects the flow of water upwards, so that on the flood the Race lies SE of the Bill and vice versa on the ebb. Conditions deteriorate with wind-against-tide, especially at springs; in an E'ly gale wind over the flood stream the Race may spread eastward to The Shambles bank. The Race normally extends about 2M S of the Bill, but further S in bad weather.

The Tidal Stream chartlets at 9.2.8 show the approx hourly positions of the Race. They are referenced to HW Portland, for the convenience of those leaving or making for Portland/Weymouth; and to HW Dover for those on passage S of the Bill. The smaller scale chartlets at 9.2.3 show the English Chan streams referenced to HW at Dover and Portsmouth.

Small craft may avoid the Race either by passing clear to seaward of it, between 3 and 5M S of the Bill; or by using the inshore passage if conditions suit. This passage is a stretch of relatively smooth water between 1ca and 3ca off the Bill (depending on wind), which should not however be used at night under power due to lobster pots. Timing is important to catch "slackish" water around the Bill, i.e:

Westbound = from HW Dover – 1 to HW + 2
(HW Portland + 4 to HW – 6).
Eastbound = from HW Dover + 5 to HW – 4
(HW Portland – 3 to HW + 1).

From either direction, close Portland at least 2M N of the Bill to utilise the S-going stream; once round the Bill, the N-going stream will set a yacht away from the Race area.

PORTLAND TO CHRISTCHURCH BAY (chart *2615*) The Shambles bank is about 3M E of Portland Bill, and should be avoided at all times. In bad weather the sea breaks heavily on it. It is marked by buoys on its E side and at SW end. E of Weymouth are rky ledges extending 3ca offshore as far as Lulworth Cove, which provides a reasonable anch in fine, settled weather and offshore winds; as do Worbarrow Bay and Chapman's Pool (9.2.10).

A firing range extends 5M offshore between Lulworth and St Alban's Hd. Yachts must pass through this area as quickly as possible, when the range is in use, see 9.2.10. Beware Kimmeridge Ledges, which extend over 5ca seaward.

St Alban's Head (107m and conspic) is steep-to and has a dangerous race off it which may extend 3M seaward. The race lies to the E on the flood and to the W on the ebb; the latter is the more dangerous. A narrow passage, at most 5ca wide and very close inshore, avoids the worst of the overfalls. There is an eddy on W side of St Alban's Head, where the stream runs almost continuously SE. 1M S of St Alban's Head the ESE stream begins at HW Portsmouth + 0520, and the WNW stream at HW –0030, with sp rates of 4·75kn.

There is deep water quite close inshore between St Alban's Hd and Anvil Pt (lt). 1M NE of Durlston Hd, Peveril Ledge runs 2½ca seaward, causing quite a bad race which extends nearly 1M eastwards, particularly on W-going stream against a SW wind. Proceeding towards the excellent shelter of Poole Harbour (9.2.13), overfalls may be met off Ballard Pt and Old Harry on the W-going stream. Studland Bay (9.2.11 and chart 2172) is a good anch especially in NW to S winds. Anch about 4ca WNW of Handfast Pt. Avoid foul areas on chart.

Poole Bay offers good sailing in waters sheltered from W and N winds, with no dangers to worry the average yacht. Tidal streams are weak N of a line between Handfast Pt and Hengistbury Hd and within Christchurch Bay. Hengistbury Hd is a dark headland, S of Christchurch hbr (9.2.14), with a groyne extending 1ca S and Beerpan Rks a further 100m E of groyne. Beware lobster pots in this area. Christchurch Ledge extends 2·75M SE from Hengistbury Hd. The tide runs hard over the ledge at sp, and there may be overfalls.

Extract V – Harbour and Anchorages: Lulworth Cove to Chapman's Pool

LULWORTH COVE, Dorset, **50°37'·00N 02°14'·82W**. AC *2172*. HW –0449 on Dover, see 9.2.7. Tides; ML 1·2m. Good shelter in fair weather and offshore winds, but heavy swell enters the cove in S and SW winds; if strong the ⚓ becomes untenable. Enter the cove slightly E of centre. A Y mooring buoy for the range safety launch is in the middle in about 4m. ⚓ in NE part in 2·5m. Holding is poor. 8kn speed limit. Local moorings, village and slip are on W side. Facilities: EC Wed/Sat; FW at tap in car park, Bar, ✉, R, Slip.

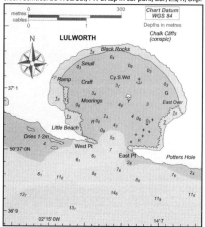

WORBARROW BAY, Dorset, **50°37'·03N 02°12'·08W**. AC *2172*. Tides as Lulworth Cove/Mupe Bay, see 9.2.7. Worbarrow is a 1½M wide bay, close E of Lulworth Cove. It is easily identified from seaward by the V-shaped gap in the hills at Arish Mell, centre of bay just E of Bindon Hill. Bindon Hill also has a white chalk scar due to cliff falls. Caution: Mupe Rks at W end and other rks 1ca off NW side. ⚓s in about 3m sheltered from W or E winds at appropriate end. The bay lies within Lulworth Ranges (see above); landing prohib at Arish Mell. No lights/facilities.

CHAPMAN'S POOL, Dorset, **50°35'·53N 02°03'·93W**. AC *2172*. Tidal data: interpolate between Mupe Bay (9.2.7) and Swanage (9. 2.11). Chapman's Pool, like Worbarrow Bay, Brandy Bay and Kimmeridge Bay, is picturesque and convenient when the wind is off-shore. ⚓ in depths of about 3m in centre of bay to avoid tidal swirl, but beware large unlit Y buoy (for Range Safety boat). From here to St Alban's Hd the stream runs SSE almost continuously due to a back eddy. No lights or facilities.